EXPANDED EDITION

OVER 150 DELICIOUS DRINKS
FOR THE HOME MIXOLOGIST

SHANE CARLEY

CIDER MILL PRESS

BOOK
PUBLISHERS
KENNEBUNKPORT, MAINE

Mason Jar Cocktails
EXPANDED EDITION

13-Digit ISBN: 978-1-64643-249-3
10-Digit ISBN: 1-64643-249-5

This book may be ordered by mail from the publisher. Please include $5.99 for postage and handling. Please support your local bookseller first!

Books published by Cider Mill Press Book Publishers are available at special discounts for bulk purchases in the United States by corporations, institutions, and other organizations. For more information, please contact the publisher.

Cider Mill Press Book Publishers
"Where good books are ready for press"
12 Spring Street
PO Box 454
Kennebunkport, Maine 04046

Visit us online!
cidermillpress.com

Typography: Brandon Grotesque, Mojito Rough

Image credits: Images on pages 20, 23, 28, 31, 32, 34, 70, 89, 101, 122, 132, 138, 146, 151, 154, 170, 177, 181, 220, 248, 252, 270, and 278 courtesy of Cider Mill Press.
All other images used under official license from Shutterstock.com.

Printed in China

Front cover image: Raspberry Margarita, see page 126
Back cover image: Peach Gin Tea, see page 189
Front endpaper image: Strawberry Gin Mojito, see page 193
Back endpaper image: Iced Coffee Explosion, see page 269

1 2 3 4 5 6 7 8 9 0
First Edition

CONTENTS

INTRODUCTION

Some drinks might call for a Collins glass. Others for a highball glass, or an Old Fashioned glass. To the average person, the subtle differences in glassware mean nothing. After all, most people aren't stocking a full bar. They're just looking for something to relax with at the end of a long day, or a way to entertain a few guests. Not only are Mason jars readily available and easy to repurpose, but they are an increasingly popular way to add a dash of personality to any cocktail you serve. *Mason Jar Cocktails Expanded Edition* offers something for anyone interested in joining the fast-growing Mason jar cocktail trend.

Mason jars cocktails are the ultimate patio drink. Whether you're mixing up a batch of sangria for the girls or just infusing a little basil lemonade for yourself, Mason jars are the ideal vessel for any refreshing drink. Whether you're chilling a glass in the freezer, or adding hot tea or coffee to your drink, a Mason jar can take it. So, forget boring old glasses. Use what you have around you and add a little charm to your drinking routine.

Some cocktails can be made in large quantities simply by multiplying the ingredient quantities. Others, not so much. If you're throwing a party and want something easy to mix up and pour in a punch bowl, look out for the Crowd-Pleaser recipes throughout this book. In addition, for those who love cocktails but aren't always interested in feeling the buzz, a selection of virgin cocktails has been included throughout the book. Look for the telltale "V" symbol that sets them apart!

VODKA-BASED COCKTAILS

Vodka is a liquor that needs no introduction. Perhaps the most common cocktail ingredient, due to its unmatched adaptability, vodka has the enviable characteristic of blending in with just about any other ingredient you throw at it. The list of vodka cocktails is vast and varied, ranging from the fruity and colorful Blue Lagoon to the creamy, sweet White Russian.

Vodka has its advantages when it comes to presentation as well. Any particularly bright ingredient like grenadine or blue curaçao will shine through its clear vodka base, enabling vodka drinks to showcase an eye-catching visual element that other alcohols simply can't match. And while gin or tequila might threaten to overwhelm any fruit garnishes with a flavor of their own, vodka often proves to be the perfect accent to anything left to set inside it.

In fact, when it comes to vodka and fruit, you may not need a cocktail at all. Why not simply soak your fruit in vodka overnight? A bowl of vodka-infused watermelon is the perfect boozy accent piece for the snack tray at any party.

The versatility of vodka is perfect for Mason jar cocktails. Mason jars can give a rustic edge to a high-class drink like the Vineyard Splash or serve as a fittingly homespun vessel for a vodka lemonade variant. Whether you're pouring drinks for yourself or showing off for a party, the following selection of vodka cocktails makes perfect use of the adaptability of both the liquor and the jar.

MAKES 1 SERVING.

Vineyard Splash

While grape-flavored beverages sometimes earn a negative reputation due to their processed flavor, fresh grapes can add a delicious and natural feel to any drink. In the case of the Vineyard Splash, you'll be making use of a grape puree, sweetened with that most adaptable of citrus fruits, lime. And why not try garnishing it with something similarly fruity and delicious, like fresh watermelon? In fact, for some added flavor, why not try adding a bit of watermelon to your puree?

1 part purple grape and watermelon puree

1 part vodka

½ lime (juiced)

1 tsp sugar

1 splash club soda

1 handful watermelon wedges (garnish)

1 If making your puree from scratch, add about 4 oz of fresh purple grapes to a food processor, along with juice from ½ lime. Add in a few small slices of fresh watermelon and blend until smooth.

2 Rim the edge of your Mason jar with the sugar if desired, then add your desired amount of ice. Add the vodka and lime juice, then pour in the grape puree. Sprinkle in the sugar and stir thoroughly.

3 Top with a splash of club soda. Stick some watermelon on a toothpick as a garnish and enjoy!

VARIATION

For a bit of natural sweetness, use green grapes instead of purple grapes. But stick with purple grapes, of course, if you want purple coloring.

Watermelon Vodka Refresher

Watermelon is an underappreciated flavor. After all, when you were a kid, wasn't watermelon the greatest flavor of freeze pop? Weren't watermelon hard candies the ones you wanted the most? Recapture a little of that nostalgia with this sweet, watermelon-flavored refresher for the hottest summer days. With a little bit of lemon juice to add a citrus kick, this is sure to be a hit, whether you're hosting a cookout or just looking to cool off.

1 part watermelon puree

1 part vodka

1 lemon (juiced)

1 tsp sugar

1 splash club soda

1 lemon slice (garnish)

1 If using fresh watermelon, add to your blender and puree.

2 Combine the vodka, pureed watermelon, and lemon juice in your Mason jar.

3 Add the sugar and stir until thoroughly mixed. Top with a splash of club soda.

4 Garnish with a slice of lemon and enjoy!

VARIATIONS

For a Frozen Watermelon Vodka Refresher, add some ice, skip the club soda, and blend the ingredients together. You'll enjoy a similar flavor with just a little extra thickness. For a virgin version of this frozen drink, skip the vodka and use more watermelon.

White Russian

Few cocktails include milk or cream, so the White Russian is a welcome departure from the norm. Already a popular drink in its own right, the White Russian was made famous by Jeff Bridges's character in "The Big Lebowski." The White Russian has a welcome smoothness to it, with none of the harsh citrus bite that most vodka drinks tend to have. Put a fun, personalized spin on this one by dropping in a cinnamon stick or two!

1 part vodka

1 part coffee liqueur

3 parts milk

Dusting of nutmeg (garnish)

1 or 2 cinnamon sticks (garnish)

1 Add the vodka, coffee liqueur, and milk to an ice-filled cocktail shaker and shake vigorously.

2 Add ice to your Mason jar and strain the shaker into it.

3 Garnish with a dusting of nutmeg and a cinnamon stick or two and enjoy!

VARIATIONS

+ **Rich White Russian:** The White Russian is traditionally made with cream rather than milk, but if you're making a larger drink, it can be difficult to stomach. If you don't mind a little added richness, go with the cream!

+ **Dirty Russian:** Made with chocolate milk.

+ **White Canadian:** Made with goat's milk in lieu of cream.

+ **White Mexican:** Made with horchata in lieu of cream.

+ **White Cuban:** Made with rum in lieu of vodka.

Mason Jar Screwdriver

Although the Screwdriver was originally created as part of a marketing ploy for Smirnoff, it has become one of the simplest and most popular drinks in the world. Featuring a bit more kick than a Mimosa, the Screwdriver is a favorite of brunchers everywhere and is the perfect midmorning drink for a lazy Saturday. Add a unique twist to your Screwdriver by rubbing a bit of pomegranate juice on the rim of your Mason jar. This will add a sharp bite of flavor to spice up your drink!

1 part vodka

2 parts orange juice

1 splash pomegranate juice (for rimming)

1 orange slice (garnish)

1 Fill your Mason jar with ice. Add the vodka and top off with orange juice.

2 Dab your finger with a bit of the pomegranate juice and rub it along the edge of the jar.

3 Garnish with an orange slice (if you're feeling fancy) and enjoy!

VARIATIONS

Any type of alcohol can be mixed with orange juice, and most of these adaptations inevitably take the name of the country for which the chosen liquor is best known. Depending on your choice of alcohol, you might find yourself making an **American Screwdriver** (bourbon), **Mexican Screwdriver** (tequila), **Cuban Screwdriver** (rum), **German Screwdriver** (schnapps), or any one of a dozen others.

CROWD-PLEASER

The Screwdriver is an ideal drink for whipping up in large batches. Just pick up a carton or two of orange juice and a bottle of vodka and combine them in a large punch bowl! For a festive look, float some pineapple wheels or maraschino cherries among the ice in the bowl.

Creamsicle

The Creamsicle is a delightful, boozy concoction that recreates all the best parts of your favorite childhood treat. A bit more complicated than the standard Screwdriver, the Creamsicle is made specifically with vanilla vodka and adds a bit of cream for a more substantial feel.

2 parts vanilla vodka

1 part orange liqueur

2 parts orange juice

2 parts half-and-half

1 orange slice (garnish)

1 Fill a mixing glass with ice. Pour in the vanilla vodka and orange liqueur, then fill the remainder with equal parts orange juice and half-and-half. Mix thoroughly.

2 Fill your Mason jar with ice as desired, then strain the mixture into it.

3 Garnish with an orange slice and enjoy!

VARIATION

Frozen Creamsicle: Simply replace the orange juice with orange sherbet and the half-and-half with vanilla ice cream, throw it in a blender with enough ice to reach your desired consistency, and blend it up!

For fruity drinks like the Creamsicle or the Screwdriver, add extra fruit slices to dress up your drink. Cut yourself some orange wheels and press them to the inside of your Mason jar when you fill it with ice, to add a colorful bit of whimsy to your drink. The best part? That fruit will be sitting there soaking up alcohol, giving you a delicious, boozy snack when your drink is gone.

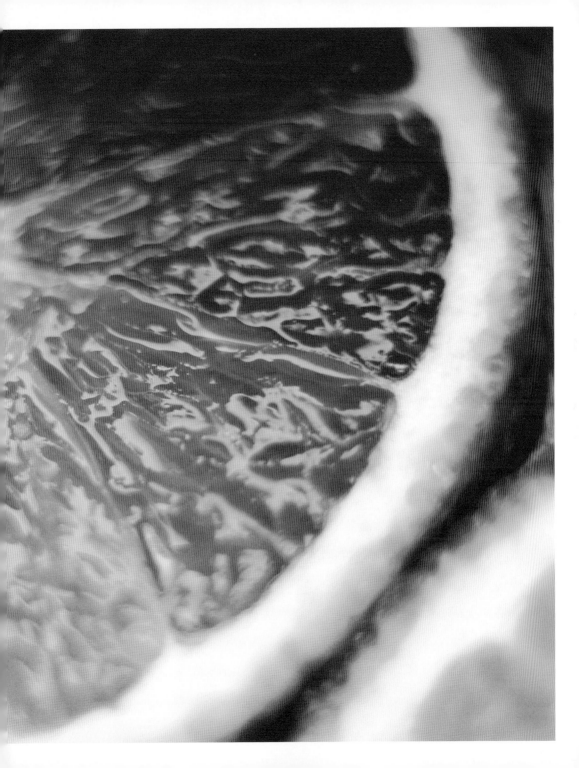

Hairy Navel

Taking its name from peach fuzz and navel oranges, the Hairy Navel combines those two delicious fruit flavors into a refreshing (and surprisingly strong) cocktail. The Mason jar version enjoys the added flavor of a small splash of pineapple juice! Although the drink contains two full shots of liquor, you wouldn't know it from the taste. You don't want to lose track of how many of these you've had—you might find yourself waking up in the yard!

1.5 oz vodka

1.5 oz peach schnapps

4 oz orange juice

1 splash pineapple juice

1 orange slice (garnish)

1 Fill your Mason jar with your desired amount of ice, then mix the vodka and peach schnapps together.

2 Top off with the orange juice and add a small splash of pineapple juice for flavor.

3 Garnish with an orange slice (or an orange wheel, if you're feeling fancy) and enjoy!

VARIATION

The **Fuzzy Navel** is a less boozy version that skips the vodka.

Mason Jar Fuzzless Navel

A nonalcoholic version of the Fuzzy Navel and Hairy Navel drinks (see page 21), the Fuzzless Navel skips the booze but leaves the flavor. If you're looking for something a bit less low-key to relax with on the porch after work, this will give you all the peachy, orangey flavor you're looking for, without the guilt that comes with drinking two shots of alcohol on a weekday.

1 part peach nectar

3 parts orange juice

1 orange slice (garnish)

1 maraschino cherry (garnish)

1 Chill your Mason jar. This step is optional, but it pays to keep a Mason jar or two in the freezer for just such an occasion.

2 Add the peach nectar, then top off with the orange juice.

3 Garnish with a slice of orange and a maraschino cherry. Enjoy!

VARIATION

If you don't have peach nectar, you can always just substitute peach juice. You will probably want to compensate by adding a bit more of it, though, as the flavor won't be as strong.

MAKES 1 SERVING.

Lemonade Shocker

The Lemonade Shocker takes the most standard of summer beverages and adds an electric splash of color and a healthy dose of booze. The Lemonade Shocker aims to appeal to both the eye and the palate. You won't scare away any less adventurous party guests either; the Lemonade Shocker tastes so much like lemonade that you might forget you're drinking a cocktail at all!

2 oz vodka

1 oz blue curaçao

2 oz lemon juice

2 oz club soda

1 lemon slice (garnish)

1 Add ice to your Mason jar.

2 Pour in the vodka, blue curaçao, and lemon juice. Stir thoroughly.

3 Top with the club soda. Add a lemon slice as a garnish and enjoy!

If you're interested in adding a bit more flavor, you can try including orange liqueur or sweet and sour mix. But I like to keep things simple.

Blue Lagoon

The Blue Lagoon is often cited as the creation of famous painter Paul Gauguin, although the truth behind the story is a subject of much debate. The vivid color of the drink is certainly worthy of an artist—the brightness of the lemonade plays nicely off the blue curaçao, giving the drink the electric blue coloration from which it takes its name. For a little more flavor, add in an extra splash of lime juice.

1 part vodka

1 part blue curaçao

4 parts lemonade

1 splash lime juice

1 lemon slice (garnish)

1 maraschino cherry (garnish)

1 Pour the vodka and blue curaçao into a cocktail shaker filled with ice and shake well.

2 Fill your Mason jar with your desired amount of ice and strain the mixture into it. Top with the lemonade and add a splash of lime juice.

3 Garnish with a slice of lemon and a maraschino cherry and enjoy!

VARIATION

If you feel that the flavor of the lemonade is too overpowering, try adding a small splash of lime cordial to introduce some variety to the drink's citrus base.

CROWD-PLEASER

The Blue Lagoon is a perfect cocktail for whipping up in large batches. Serve from a large glass jug on the refreshments table, with lemon slices and maraschino cherries on the side.

Virgin Blue Lagoon

While the regular Blue Lagoon gets its color from blue curaçao, the virgin option has to be a bit more creative. The Virgin Blue Lagoon takes on a smoothie-like consistency, featuring fresh fruit, yogurt, and a fun dash of whipped cream.

½ cup vanilla yogurt

½ cup blueberries

½ cup ice (recommended)

Whipped cream as desired

1 lemon slice (garnish)

1 maraschino cherry (garnish)

1 Pour the vanilla yogurt and blueberries into a blender. Add the ice and blend until smooth.

2 Pour into your Mason jar and top with the whipped cream.

3 Garnish your jar with a lemon slice and a maraschino cherry and enjoy!

VARIATION

For a slightly different consistency, consider using ice cream instead of yogurt.

Citrus Sunset

Made primarily with grapefruit juice, lime, and lemon juice, the Citrus Sunset is a sweet-and-sour assault on your taste buds that will leave your mouth watering. With its beautiful presentation, the Citrus Sunset is a great way to steal the attention of your guests' eyes as well as their appetites.

1 part vodka

4 parts grapefruit juice

½ lime (juiced)

¼ lemon (juiced)

1 splash grenadine

1 lime slice (garnish)

1 Add your desired amount of ice to your Mason jar, then add the vodka and grapefruit juice. Squeeze in the juice of half a lime and a quarter of a lemon and stir until mixed.

2 Pour a splash of grenadine into the middle of the drink, allowing it to sink straight to the bottom. This should create a subtle layering effect with the grapefruit juice.

3 Garnish with a slice of lime and enjoy!

Melon Ball

Typically garnished with the fruit snack from which it takes its name, the Melon Ball makes use of an underutilized fruit flavor. Veering away from the all-too-common choices of limoncello or triple sec, the Melon Ball instead opts for the subtler flavor of melon liqueur. This Mason jar version also includes a small splash of lime juice to add a bit more complexity of flavor. Melon ballers aren't exactly the most common kitchen utensil these days, but if you want to make your Melon Ball right, you'll need one. Although garnishes usually aren't completely necessary, in this case it just doesn't seem right to serve the drink without including its namesake.

1 part vodka

2 parts melon liqueur

4 parts pineapple juice

1 splash lime juice

Melon balls as desired (garnish)

1 Add the ingredients (except the melon balls for garnish) to an ice-filled cocktail shaker and shake well.

2 Fill your Mason jar with ice, add some melon balls, and strain the cocktail in. Enjoy!

VARIATION

Frozen Melon Ball: Add a cup or two of ice, and blend the ingredients instead of shaking.

There is considerable disagreement about the ingredients of the basic Melon Ball; while pineapple juice is the most popular variant, many believe that orange juice should be used instead. Both versions appear to have equal claim to the name.

Moscow Mule

Though it was only made popular after a particularly successful Smirnoff ad campaign, the Moscow Mule has supposedly been around for nearly a century. In all that time, it hasn't changed much at all. After all, why would it? The Moscow Mule is as simple as drinks come, featuring just two primary ingredients and that ever-present cocktail standby, a splash of citrus. In this case, let's modify it just a bit by adding a bite of flavor in the form of a few mint leaves.

4 mint leaves

½ lime (juiced)

1 part vodka

3 parts ginger beer

1 lime wedge

1 Add the mint leaves to the bottom of your Mason jar, then juice the half lime into the jar. Add your desired amount of ice atop the juice.

2 Pour in the vodka and top off with the ginger beer.

3 Garnish with a wedge of lime and enjoy!

VARIATION

Mexican Mule: Made with tequila rather than vodka (page 150).

Right about now, some cocktail aficionados are probably saying, "Hey, isn't the Moscow Mule supposed to be served in a copper mug?" While that's true, let's be honest: How many among us actually own a copper mug? The truth is, most cocktails are simply served in whatever glassware is at hand. The growing popularity of the Mason jar offers most drinkers a handy way to incorporate a little rustic charm.

MAKES 1 SERVING.

Virgin Mule

Sometimes the simplest things in life are best. The Virgin Mule proves that replacing liquor lost can be pointless. When you've already got a delicious cocktail sitting in front of you, why do any more than skip the booze? Some beverages don't need much more than a healthy dose of lime to take them to the next level, and ginger beer is one such beverage.

½ lime (juiced)

6 oz ginger beer

1 lime wedge (garnish)

1 Juice half of a lime into your Mason jar. Add your desired amount of ice.

2 Top off with the ginger beer.

3 Garnish with a wedge of lime and enjoy!

Fun fact: the Mason jar was invented and patented by John Landis Mason in 1858.

Melon Refresher

When it comes to entertaining a large group of people, you want the cocktails you serve to impress, but you also want them to be simple to make. If a simple spiked punch isn't for you, try this quick and easy Melon Refresher. Little more than a vodka drink with a welcome splash of melon, this will please all but the most difficult cocktail snob. The Mason jar presentation only adds to the modest and effortless atmosphere you're cultivating.

1 part melon liqueur

1 part vodka

4 parts lemon-lime soda

1 lime wheel (garnish)

1 Add ice to your Mason jar, then pour in the melon liqueur and vodka.

2 Top off with your favorite lemon-lime soda.

3 Garnish with a lime wheel and enjoy!

Lime juice plays well off of just about any other fruit flavor, so if you want to hit this drink with a little extra lime juice, go right ahead.

Mason Jar Bloody Mary

More than any other drink, the Bloody Mary has come to be known as a hangover cure. It's a morning drink with a bit more substance than a Mimosa, with enough tasty ingredients to drown out the vodka. Bars and pubs seem to be on a never-ending quest to one-up each other in the Bloody Mary department, creating increasingly outlandish garnishes until the drink itself becomes almost an afterthought. There's no need for that. Keep it simple. The Bloody Mary is the perfect way to get your weekend started and give you the fortitude you need to face the day.

Old Bay seasoning
(for rimming)

1 lime wedge (juiced)

2 oz vodka

½ oz olive juice

2 dashes horseradish

Tomato juice to fill

3 drops Worcestershire sauce

3 dashes hot sauce

1 dash black pepper

2 dashes celery salt

Garnish options: 1 celery stick, a rasher of cooked bacon, or 3 olives—or all of 'em!

1 Rim the edge of your Mason jar with the Old Bay seasoning (use juice from the lime wedge as the binding agent).

2 Add the vodka, olive juice, lime juice, and horseradish into your jar, along with a handful of ice cubes. Top with the tomato juice, leaving enough space to stir, and mix thoroughly.

3 Add the Worcestershire sauce, hot sauce, pepper, and celery salt. Stir again until mixed.

4 Garnish with one large celery stick, a rasher of crispy bacon, or three olives (put them on a toothpick and eat them at your leisure)—whichever of these fixin's you prefer. Enjoy!

VARIATIONS

Bloody Mary variations are too numerous to count, but most of them center on the garnishes. The more common garnishes include celery, bacon, olives, cocktail onions, pickles, pepperoncini, garlic, lemon, and chili peppers. On the other hand, some of the more over-the-top garnishes vary from onion rings all the way up to entire cheeseburgers, or even (in one particularly inspired and upscale establishment) foie gras.

Mason Jar Virgin Mary

If you're in favor of tomato juice and you like to keep things spicy, you're probably a big Bloody Mary fan. But starting the day off with a heaping helping of vodka might not always agree with you, so why not give this nonalcoholic version a try? The Virgin Mary combines all the things you love best about a Bloody Mary (lots of tomato juice, a horseradish kick, and, of course, outrageous garnishes) and strips away the unwanted booze, leaving you with what actually ends up being a pretty healthy way to start your morning.

Cracked black pepper
(for rimming)

1 lime wedge (juiced)

½ oz olive juice

2 dashes horseradish

Tomato juice to fill

3 drops Worcestershire sauce

3 dashes hot sauce

1 dash black pepper

2 dashes celery salt

1 celery stick (garnish)

1 handful chili peppers
(garnish)

1 Rim the edge of your Mason jar with the cracked black pepper (use juice from the lime wedge as the binding agent).

2 Add the olive juice, lime juice, and horseradish into your jar, along with a handful of ice cubes. Top with the tomato juice, leaving enough space to stir, and mix thoroughly.

3 Add the Worcestershire sauce, hot sauce, pepper, and celery salt. Stir again until mixed.

4 Garnish with one large celery stick and a handful of bright red chili peppers. Enjoy!

VARIATIONS

As with the standard Bloody Mary, experiment with ingredients and garnishes at your leisure. A wide variety of meats and vegetables (especially spicy ones) go extremely well with the Virgin Mary drink, so try all of your favorites.

Vanilla Pear

By now you've likely tried drinks made with lemon juice, lime juice, apple juice, cranberry juice, and maybe even grapefruit juice or pineapple juice. But what about pear juice? It might not be at the top of your shopping list, but the subtle flavor of pear can add unusual and enticing notes to any cocktail. In the case of the Vanilla Pear, the pear juice is complemented by the similarly understated vanilla vodka. A drop of almond extract adds just a hint of almond flavor, which pairs extremely well with both.

Sugar (for rimming)

2 parts pear juice

1 part vanilla vodka

1 drop almond extract

1 pear wheel (garnish)

1 Rim the edge of your Mason jar with the sugar and add ice.

2 Pour the pear juice and vanilla vodka into a cocktail shaker filled with ice. Add almond extract and shake vigorously until mixed.

3 Add the vodka mixture to your Mason jar. Garnish with a pear wheel (deseeded, of course) and enjoy!

VARIATION

If you don't have vanilla vodka, you can use a tiny bit of vanilla extract to achieve similar results. Be careful, though: too much vanilla extract can be not only overwhelming, but unappetizing as well.

Rimming a jar is easy: Simply rub a lemon or a lime on the glass (even water will do, if you don't want any citrus flavor) and turn it over into a dish of salt or sugar. But when it comes to rimming a jar with something more substantial, you'll need more adhesiveness than water or lemon juice can provide. Try rubbing a bit of honey on the edge instead. It's much stickier and adds another layer of flavor to boot!

Strawberry Cream Shake

Mixing ice cream and alcohol is a time-honored summer tradition. But plain old vanilla ice cream is so boring—so why not add some strawberry? Already among vodka's most delicious flavor variations, the addition of a little fresh strawberry to vanilla ice cream and milk creates a strawberries-and-cream medley as tasty as anything you've ever had!

3 strawberries (hulled)

6 oz vanilla ice cream

1 oz milk

1 oz strawberry vodka

1 oz vanilla vodka

1 dollop whipped cream (garnish)

1 Add the strawberries to a blender and puree. Add the vanilla ice cream, milk, and both vodkas, and blend again until smooth. Pour the mixture into your Mason jar.

2 Top with a dollop of whipped cream. If you have extra strawberries, stick one on the rim of the jar as a garnish and enjoy!

VARIATIONS

Try it with your favorite type of ice cream! Experiment with different vodka flavors too. You can even throw in some other liqueurs to mix flavors—chocolate and cherry, cranberry and orange, or any other combo that suits you.

Mason Jar Mudslide

The Mudslide is almost a chocolate/coffee milk shake, with a significant kick of alcohol. It's an incredibly rich cocktail, sporting heavy cream on top of Irish cream, plus chocolate and coffee flavors. You probably won't want to have more than one of these at a time. But that's okay, because one is enough. The standard Mudslide contains about two shots of liquor in total, although experienced Mudslide drinkers have a tendency to boost the alcohol content skyward. For the Mason jar version, try adding a colorful sprig of mint to put a unique twist on this classic!

1 oz vodka

1 oz coffee liqueur

1 oz Irish cream

1 oz heavy cream

1 cup ice

Chocolate syrup (garnish)

Whipped cream (garnish)

1 mint sprig (garnish)

1 Add the vodka, coffee liqueur, Irish cream, heavy cream, and ice to your blender and blend until it reaches the desired consistency. For a more chocolatey taste, feel free to add a dash of chocolate syrup to the blender as well.

2 Pour the resulting concoction into your Mason jar. Top with whipped cream and drizzle some chocolate syrup for an extra bit of flair, then add a mint sprig for color. Enjoy!

VARIATIONS

+ Although the Mudslide is already "frozen" by most drink standards, you can give it an even more milk shake–like consistency by swapping out the heavy cream for three times the amount of vanilla ice cream and eliminating the ice. To give your drink a bit more volume, you might want to double the recipe (2 oz of each alcohol, 6 oz of ice cream), but be aware that this will create a *much* stronger cocktail.

+ Garnish with shaved chocolate, or even top the drink with a strawberry to add a fruity zing.

Virgin Mudslide

When you get right down to it, this Virgin Mudslide is a glitzy chocolate milk shake. It's the perfect dessert cocktail for a night where you want to keep a clear head but don't want to miss out on all the fun.

1 dash shaved chocolate
(for rimming)

1 oz cream

2 or 3 scoops vanilla ice cream

1 splash Amaretto syrup

Chocolate syrup as desired

Whipped cream (garnish)

1 maraschino cherry (garnish)

1 Rim the edge of your Mason jar with the shaved chocolate—use some of the vanilla ice cream as your binding agent.

2 Add the cream and vanilla ice cream to a blender and blend until mixed.

3 Add the Amaretto syrup and your desired amount of chocolate syrup to the blended mixture. Blend again until thoroughly mixed.

4 Pour the Mudslide into your Mason jar. Top with whipped cream and sprinkle with some leftover shaved chocolate. Add a maraschino cherry for a final touch and enjoy!

VARIATIONS

+ Don't feel married to the amounts prescribed here. Adding extra cream or milk will thin out your Mudslide, while adding more ice cream will thicken it up. It all comes down to personal preference, so feel free to experiment!

+ Some Virgin Mudslide recipes call for the addition of a splash of hazelnut syrup. If you're a fan of hazelnut (especially in your coffee), try it out.

Old-Fashioned Apple Pie

Apple pie is one of the signature flavors of fall, so it only makes sense to try to capture all its glory in cocktail form. The Old-Fashioned Apple Pie might not be as good as what your grandma makes, but it will keep you warm when the weather turns crisp. After all, patio season shouldn't have to end just because it's getting a little colder outside, should it?

1 part vanilla vodka

1 dash brown sugar

2 parts apple cider

2 parts apple juice

1 dash cinnamon

1 Pour the vanilla vodka into your Mason jar and add a dash of brown sugar. Stir until mostly dissolved.

2 Add the apple cider and apple juice with a dash of cinnamon. Stir again. Enjoy!

VARIATIONS

+ Serve with a dollop of whipped cream and a cinnamon stick or two.

+ This drink can be served hot or cold. If you want to heat it, try simmering the ingredients after combining them. Feel free to experiment with other spices too! If you choose to heat your drink, watch out; the Mason jar will get hot.

Arctic Warmer

What do you do when the weather turns cold, and you don't know what to do with all that extra vodka and tequila you've got lying around? You make a winter warmer with it, of course. Not every cocktail has to be crisp and cool, and the Arctic Warmer is the perfect example of why. Heat up some of your favorite tea, and make sure you don't burn yourself!

4 parts hot tea

Butter to taste

2 parts vodka

1 part tequila

1 dash cinnamon

1 or 2 cinnamon sticks
(garnish)

1 Use one tea bag to make a serving of your favorite tea in your Mason jar. Melt a small pat of butter into the tea.

2 Add the vodka, tequila, and cinnamon and stir until thoroughly mixed.

3 Garnish with a cinnamon stick or two and enjoy!

If you don't like the idea of butter in a beverage, you can substitute cream or milk. Just be aware that this will change the flavor of the drink quite a bit. Butter is best.

46 | MASON JAR COCKTAILS EXPANDED EDITION

MAKES 1 SERVING.

Gingerbread Whisper

Most winter cocktails tend to be of the "warmer" variety, and while there is something cozy about sipping a warm hot chocolate spiked with whiskey or rum, traditional cocktails have their place during the snowy season as well. The Gingerbread Whisper incorporates the uniquely wintery flavor of gingerbread with the richness of Irish cream to create a cocktail that will warm you in a slightly different way.

1 oz gingerbread vodka

4 oz Irish cream liqueur

Dusting of nutmeg (garnish)

1 Add ice to your Mason jar and pour in the gingerbread vodka and liqueur. Stir until thoroughly combined.

2 Top with a dusting of nutmeg if desired and enjoy!

VARIATION

For a fall version, replace the gingerbread vodka with pumpkin vodka. You can also use regular vodka and replace the Irish cream liqueur with a pumpkin cream liqueur. See which version you like better!

MAKES 1 SERVING.

Mason Jar Sea Breeze

Aptly named after the perfect environment in which to consume it, the Sea Breeze offers a delicious mix of fruit flavors built over an unobtrusive vodka base. Cranberry and grapefruit juice might not be the most obvious flavor combination, but the sharp bite of the vodka is the perfect complement to both. Seal up your Mason jar and take this one to the beach or a picnic as a bright and colorful summer refresher. For a fun twist, add a little splash of lime juice to provide a bit of extra citrus bite.

1 part vodka

3 parts cranberry juice

1 part grapefruit juice

1 splash lime juice

1 lime wedge (garnish)

1 Fill your Mason jar with your desired amount of ice. Add the ingredients into it (except the lime wedge for garnish).

2 Garnish with a wedge of lime and enjoy!

VARIATION

Bay Breeze: Use pineapple juice instead of grapefruit juice.

Mason jars have become such a sensation that you can find custom-made Mason jars all over the internet. Some come with handles, others with artsy, specially designed lids and glass straws, or chalkboard-style space for writing your name, or hand-painted folk art. Poke around a little, and you might find something that adds the perfect accent to your party setup!

MAKES 1 SERVING.

Raspberry Twist

Lemonade and iced tea are delicious. Raspberry iced tea is delicious. And raspberry lemonade is delicious. Why not combine all these flavors into a boozy treat that will dance the lambada across your grateful taste buds? The Raspberry Twist takes the best aspects of three popular drinks and adds a healthy dose of booze to leave you smiling on a hot summer day.

3 or 4 raspberries (garnish)

1 part raspberry vodka

2 parts lemonade

2 parts iced tea (sweetened)

1 Put ice and the raspberries in your Mason jar and add the raspberry vodka.

2 Add the lemonade and sweetened iced tea in approximately equal parts and stir until thoroughly mixed.

3 Enjoy! And don't forget to eat the booze-infused raspberries when you're done.

VARIATIONS

+ If you're really an unsweetened iced tea devotee, you can always use that instead. The drink is going to be pretty sweet anyway, though, so it probably won't make a huge difference.

+ Feel free to sub in different tea flavors. Black tea, green tea, and any other flavor you might prefer is perfectly acceptable. Of course, homemade iced tea is always going to taste best.

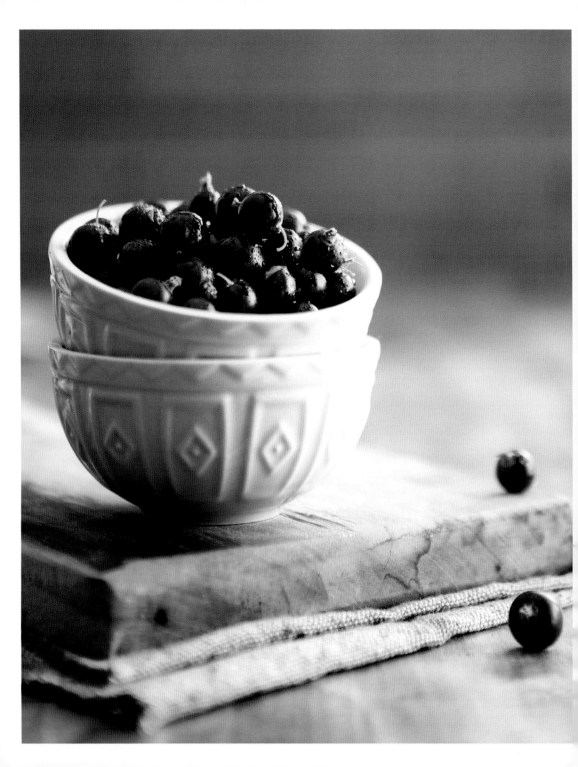

Currant Events

Blackcurrant is having a moment. Although most people have never tasted the fruit itself, blackcurrant flavoring is making its way into beer, liquor, and even wine. There's a reason for this, of course: the sweet-and-sour burst of the fruit gives it a distinctive flavor profile that pairs well with raspberry, blackberry, and more. For this particular cocktail, a splash of ginger beer at the end provides a welcome bite that complements the sweetness of the fruit.

3 oz vodka

1 oz blackcurrant liqueur

½ cup to 1 cup crushed ice

1 oz ginger beer

1 blackberry (garnish)

1 Add the vodka and blackcurrant liqueur to a cocktail shaker filled with ice. Shake vigorously.

2 Fill your Mason jar approximately halfway with crushed ice. Strain the cocktail shaker into it.

3 Top with an ounce of ginger beer and garnish with a blackberry. Enjoy!

Blueberry Brunch

Why just drink your cocktails when you can eat them too? Fresh fruit is a welcome addition to just about any vodka cocktail, and this bright and fresh lemonade-based drink is no exception. Flavored vodkas can be on the sweet side, but balancing them with fresh fruit can make a big difference. The best part? Chowing down on that boozy fruit when you're finished!

4 oz lemonade

2 oz blueberry vodka

1 splash lime juice

Fresh blueberries

Fresh lemon slices

Mint leaves (garnish)

1 Add the lemonade, blueberry vodka, and lime juice to a cocktail shaker filled with ice. Shake vigorously.

2 Fill your Mason jar approximately halfway with ice and strain the cocktail shaker into it.

3 Top with fresh blueberries and lemon slices. Garnish with one or more mint leaves and enjoy!

VARIATION

Blueberries are delicious, but you can also mix and match fruits and their corresponding vodka flavors. Fresh strawberries and strawberry vodka make a particularly enticing combination. Be creative!

MAKES 1 SERVING.

A Summer's Day

Shall I compare thee to a summer's day? This drink does compare quite favorably to the warmth and beauty of an August afternoon, combining some of the finest flavors of summer to create a drink that is both sweet and refreshing. A Summer's Day is the perfect porch sipper for a hot afternoon. Surely, Shakespeare himself would agree.

2 oz watermelon vodka

4 oz lemon-lime soda

1 oz orange liqueur

Watermelon cubes (garnish)

1 Fill your Mason jar approximately halfway with ice. Add the watermelon vodka, lemon-lime soda, and orange liqueur. Stir thoroughly.

2 Garnish with fresh watermelon cubes or slices and enjoy!

VARIATION

For some extra tartness, add a splash of lime juice to finish. Alternatively, swap out the lemon-lime soda for grapefruit soda, or a favorite flavored seltzer!

Heliopause

In astronomical terms, the heliopause represents the very edge of the sun's influence. As a cocktail, its dark coloration evokes an "end of summer" feeling, as the sun's influence begins to fade from our lives. Heliopause is a melancholic drink, one meant for sipping with a friend rather than at a party. It's an understated cocktail—but one well worth trying.

6 oz orange juice

1 oz vodka

1 oz orange liqueur

1 oz blackcurrant liqueur

1 orange wheel (garnish)

1 Add the orange juice, vodka, and orange liqueur to a cocktail shaker. Shake vigorously.

2 Strain the resulting mixture into a Mason jar filled with ice. Add the blackcurrant liqueur, but do not stir.

3 Garnish with an orange wheel if desired. Enjoy!

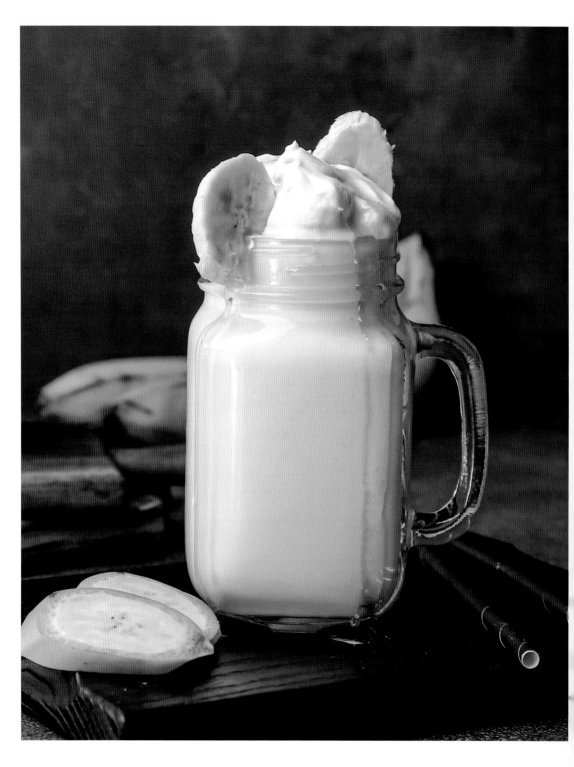

MAKES 2 SERVINGS.

Banana Party

Bananas and cream may not be as popular as peaches and cream, but rest assured that they make a delicious combination. The Banana Party combines the flavors of fresh banana and vanilla ice cream with their boozy counterparts, creating a smoothie-like cocktail perfect for any occasion. Be careful: it may not taste like it, but this cocktail can pack a punch!

1 banana

2 scoops vanilla ice cream

4 oz banana liqueur

2 oz vanilla vodka

2 cups ice (approximately 1 per serving)

Whipped cream (garnish)

1 Add the banana, vanilla ice cream, banana liqueur, vanilla vodka, and ice to a blender. Blend to your desired consistency.

2 Pour the resulting mixture into the two Mason jars. Top with whipped cream if desired and enjoy!

RUM-BASED COCKTAILS

Although it doesn't quite play off the flavor of its fellow ingredients the way vodka does, rum is a bit of a chameleon itself. Featured in the ever-popular mint Mojito as well as the fruity Piña Colada, rum doesn't try to blend in. Usable in drinks both hot and cold, the taste of rum (and its many flavored variants) provides the perfect accent for dozens of cocktails. One taste of a Mojito, and Hemingway's love of them is a mystery no more.

Light rum, dark rum, spiced rum, and flavored rum are featured in a litany of delicious recipes. Fruit daiquiris, minty concoctions, creamy refreshers, and hot, buttery warmers are just a few of the things you'll find in the following pages. Driving home the idea that rum can do just about anything, this wide range of flavor profiles and ingredients rivals even vodka's impressive spread.

One of the beautiful things about rum is that its cocktails hardly ever stand on ceremony. Rarely does a rum drink call for a cocktail glass or a champagne flute. Rum is a liquor that understands the utility of alcohol. Why dig out a Collins glass when a regular old cup will do just fine? Or, for that matter, a Mason jar? Forget using the "right" glass. If you want to enjoy a brief mental vacation with a tropical daiquiri, that cocktail umbrella will look just as fine in a Mason jar. Maybe even better.

Mason Jar Mojito

Maybe the best thing to come out of Cuba since cigars, the Mojito is one of the most popular drinks in the world. Minty drinks are always delicious, and the Mojito is so simple to make that it almost feels like cheating. White rum, a hint of mint, a splash of lime, and presto: refreshment. For full effect, be sure to get yourself a seersucker suit or a sun hat to wear while you drink.

1 tbsp sugar

½ lime (juiced)

1 cup crushed ice

10 mint leaves

2 oz white rum

6 oz club soda

3 or 6 mint sprigs (garnish)

2 or 3 lime wheels (garnish)

1 Add the sugar and fresh lime juice to your Mason jar and stir until the sugar has dissolved.

2 Add ¼ of the crushed ice, then take the mint leaves, rub them over the edge of the jar, tear each one in half, and add them on top of the ice. Stir again.

3 Add the white rum, club soda, and remaining ice. Stir one last time, then add a few mint sprigs and a lime wheel for garnish. Stick the remaining lime wheels into the drink itself for a little extra visual flair. Enjoy!

VARIATIONS

As with many popular drinks, there are countless variations of the Mojito, most centering around the primary alcohol. The **Mexican Mojito** substitutes tequila for rum, the **English Mojito** substitutes gin, the **Dirty Mojito** substitutes spiced rum, etc.

Rather than using a dash of sugar or a squirt of simple syrup, some drinks call for sugar cubes. The cubes are not intended to remain whole and take a while to dissolve in a cold drink, so they are generally used in the muddling process. Muddling sugar cubes with other ingredients can help infuse the sugar with flavor and make it more than just a sweetener.

Nojito

The Nojito (little more than a Virgin Mojito) is extremely simple to make. Eliminating the rum upon which the original Mojito is based, the Nojito swaps out the club soda for more flavorful ginger ale, giving the drink the kick that it needs. A Nojito should look almost identical to a Mojito. It won't quite taste the same, but it's a surprisingly tasty way to trick your palate when you're feeling a bit boozed out.

1 tbsp sugar

½ lime (juiced)

1 handful mint leaves

1 cup crushed ice

8 oz ginger ale

3 or 6 mint sprigs (garnish)

1 lime wheel (garnish)

1 Add the sugar and lime juice to the bottom of your Mason jar and mix until the sugar is dissolved. Muddle the mint leaves into this mixture.

2 Pour in the ice, then add the ginger ale. Garnish with mint sprigs and a lime wheel and enjoy!

Not all variations call for ginger ale. In fact, some stick to the standard club soda, with the only real difference between the Mojito and the Nojito being the elimination of the rum. This lacks flavor, though—you're essentially drinking water with lime.

MAKES 1 SERVING.

Pineapple Citrus Refresher

Pineapple and mint play off one another better than you might suspect, and with a little fizzy carbonation courtesy of the lemon-lime soda, the Pineapple Citrus Refresher will pep you right up. The best part? Eating the pineapple slices at the bottom.

2 oz simple syrup (page 190)

2 or 3 slices of pineapple

1 handful mint leaves

½ lime (juiced)

2 oz light rum

4 oz lemon-lime soda

1 mint sprig (garnish)

1 Add the simple syrup to your Mason jar, along with the pineapple slices. Muddle the pineapple slices to release the pineapple juice, and leave them in the jar. Add your desired amount of ice.

2 Rub the rim of the jar with the mint leaves, then tear them in half and leave them on top of the ice.

3 Squeeze the lime juice into the jar, then add the light rum and lemon-lime soda on top. Garnish with a sprig of mint and enjoy!

VARIATION

If club soda is too flavorless for you, you might try using ginger ale.

While professional bartenders might have a "muddling stick" or "muddling spoon," you don't need anything more complicated than the back of a regular old spoon. Simply add the necessary ingredients to a glass or a shaker and lightly mash them to release the juices and flavors. There's no need to get rough—you're not making mashed potatoes—but don't be afraid to use a heavy hand.

Caribbean Rum Punch

The basis for just about every fruity beach drink under the sun, rum is the rare liquor beloved by both creative mixologists and those who prefer it on its own merits. No matter how much you like rum, you probably shouldn't just fill a Mason jar with it, though. Instead, reach for some punch. Caribbean Rum Punch can be made in a variety of different ways, all of them delicious.

1 part silver rum

1 part coconut rum

½ lime (juiced)

1 dash bitters

2 parts orange juice

2 parts pineapple juice

2 or 3 pineapple wedges (garnish)

1 Add ice to your Mason jar, then pour in the rums and lime juice. Add a dash of bitters.

2 Pour the orange juice and pineapple juice in approximately equal parts and stir until completely mixed.

3 Garnish with a few pineapple wedges, and enjoy!

VARIATIONS

Caribbean Rum Punch is just that—a punch. As such, it can really be manipulated in any way you see fit. Don't like coconut rum? Take it out. Think cranberry juice is a better choice than pineapple juice? Make the switch! Rum is an incredibly versatile liquor, and you know your personal tastes better than anyone.

CROWD-PLEASER

The Caribbean Rum Punch drink might look like a chore to multiply into larger proportions, but it pays off. With a bottle of orange juice, a bottle of pineapple juice, and a half bottle each of silver rum and coconut rum, you'll have a drink ready to fill a punch bowl and keep your guests happy all night. Just add a little lime to taste and a few drops of bitters, and you're done! For some extra panache, add fresh fruit, like oranges, lemons, and grapes, to the punch.

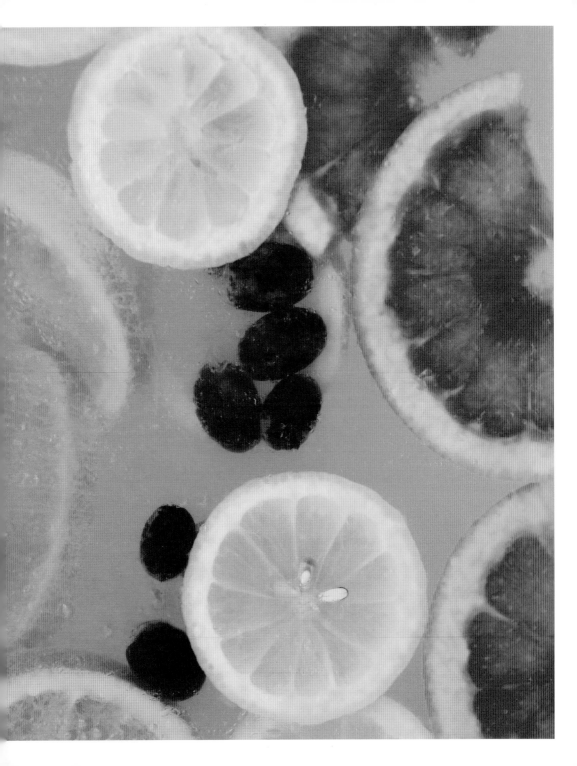

Mason Jar Mango Tango

Made with mango juice, an admittedly uncommon ingredient, the Mango Tango is a tart, boozy smoothie for hot days. The drink makes use of the contrasting flavors of dark rum and coconut rum, two favorite tropical drink ingredients. Calling for mango, pineapple, and lime juices (not to mention orange liqueur), the Mango Tango is an aggressively citrusy concoction that will pucker your face in the best possible way.

1 oz dark rum

1 oz coconut rum

1 oz orange liqueur

½ lime (juiced)

4 oz mango juice

2 oz pineapple juice

1 mango slice (garnish)

1 Pour the liquid ingredients into a blender, adding as many ice cubes as necessary to reach the desired consistency. Blend until smooth.

2 Pour the resulting smoothie into your Mason jar and garnish with a slice of mango. Enjoy!

VARIATION

Some swear that it isn't a true Mango Tango unless a Frozen Strawberry Daiquiri (page 75) is layered into the drink. The resulting cocktail displays a beautiful medley of bright oranges and reds.

Frozen Strawberry Daiquiri

The Frozen Strawberry Daiquiri is, without a doubt, the most popular drink in the daiquiri family. It isn't even close, really. You'll find Frozen Strawberry Daiquiris on the menu at just about any bar or restaurant you go to, but why pay outrageous prices when you can easily mix one up yourself? This is a drink best made in large batches, so gather a few friends and enjoy this summery treat together!

Sugar (for rimming)

6 oz light rum

2 oz orange liqueur

1 oz simple syrup (page 190)

2 limes (juiced)

2 cups fresh strawberries (hulled)

4 cups ice (about 1 cup per serving)

1 handful sliced strawberries (garnish)

1 Rim the edges of four Mason jars with the strawberries and sugar.

2 Add all the ingredients to a blender (except the strawberries for garnish) and blend until smooth. Be sure to test a few times to be sure that all the ice and strawberries have been sufficiently blended.

3 Pour the blended cocktails into the four Mason jars.

4 To dress up the presentation, slice some fresh strawberries. Either stick one or two on the edge of each jar or simply add them to each drink itself and serve with long spoons. Enjoy!

Not all Frozen Strawberry Daiquiri variants include orange liqueur, but it definitely helps balance the flavor with a tiny tang of citrus.

Virgin Strawberry Daiquiri

Like its boozy counterpart, the Virgin Strawberry Daiquiri is a tasty mix of strawberry, orange, and lime flavors in refreshing frozen form. Perfect for summer patio parties when you want to keep things low-key and under control, the Virgin Strawberry Daiquiri is a great way to ease into the weekend. Save the drinking for later and enjoy the evening while sipping a delicious fruit concoction on the porch and watching the sunset.

8 oz lemon-lime soda

2 oz orange juice

1 oz simple syrup (page 190)

2 limes (juiced)

2 cups fresh strawberries (hulled)

4 cups ice (about 1 cup per serving)

1 handful strawberries (garnish)

1 Add all the ingredients to a blender (except the strawberries for garnish) and blend until smooth. Make sure that all ice and strawberries have been sufficiently blended; it may take a few blending cycles.

2 Pour the blended cocktails into four Mason jars.

3 Add a strawberry or two to each drink or the edge of each jar as a garnish and enjoy!

When you have all the ingredients on hand to make Frozen Strawberry Daiquiris (page 75), it's simple to blend a virgin version as well. Just clean the blender between batches if you're serving kiddos.

Mason Jar Piña Colada

The love affair between rum and pineapple juice continues! Despite what the famous song says, you don't have to love getting caught in the rain to enjoy a good Piña Colada. In fact, this simple drink is the national drink of Puerto Rico, one of the sunniest places on the planet. Translating literally to "strained pineapple," the Piña Colada is a relatively new cocktail—dating back only 50 years or so—but one that has quickly gained popularity among island tourists and continental mixologists alike.

1 part white rum

1 part coconut cream

3 parts pineapple juice

½ cup to 1 cup ice

1 pineapple wedge (garnish)

1 maraschino cherry (garnish)

1 Add the white rum, coconut cream, pineapple juice, and ice to a blender and blend until smooth, adding ice as needed to achieve the desired consistency. Don't go too overboard here, as the Piña Colada doesn't need to be as thick as most frozen drinks.

2 Pour into your Mason jar and garnish with a pineapple wedge and maraschino cherry. Enjoy!

VARIATIONS

Coconut Colada: Hit the finished drink with a dusting of shaved coconut.

Lava Flow: Layer a Piña Colada and a Frozen Strawberry Daiquiri (page 75) for a colorful and delicious combination!

Virgin Piña Colada

The Piña Colada isn't a particularly strong drink in the first place, so a virgin version certainly doesn't lose much in translation. In fact, the reason the Piña Colada is so beloved is largely because of the rich flavor of the coconut cream playing off the sweet pineapple juice. Who needs rum, anyway?

1 part coconut cream

3 parts pineapple juice

½ cup to 1 cup crushed ice

1 pineapple wedge (garnish)

1 maraschino cherry (garnish)

1 Add the coconut cream, pineapple juice, and ice to a blender and blend until smooth, adding ice as needed to achieve the desired consistency. As with the regular Mason Jar Piña Colada, don't go too overboard. It doesn't need to be smoothie thick.

2 Pour into your Mason jar and garnish with a pineapple wedge and maraschino cherry. Enjoy!

VARIATION

Virgin Coconut Colada: Hit the finished drink with a dusting of shaved coconut.

Virgin Lava Flow: Try mixing a Virgin Strawberry Daiquiri (page 77) and a Virgin Piña Colada for another colorful drink that's just as tasty!

Frozen Hemingway Daiquiri

Known almost as much for his drinking ability as for his writing, Ernest Hemingway was the inspiration for (and, if the legend is to be believed, the inventor of) this fruity cocktail. Heavier on alcohol than the average daiquiri, and lighter on sugar, the Hemingway Daiquiri is famous for its novelty. Typically a sipping cocktail, it can be adapted into the Frozen Hemingway Daiquiri with the addition of just a bit of ice, giving you a frozen, smoothie-like drink that will fill both your Mason jar and your belly.

2 oz light rum

¼ oz cherry liqueur

1 oz grapefruit juice

½ lime (juiced)

1 tsp sugar

1 cup ice

1 lime wedge (garnish)

1 Using a blender or food processor, blend all the ingredients together (except the lime wedge). Adjust the amount of ice, depending on your desired consistency.

2 Pour into your Mason jar and garnish with a lime wedge. Enjoy!

While it won't yield the same crisp taste, you can always use lime juice if you don't have fresh limes handy. The average lime contains about 2 tablespoons' worth of juice, so use that as your rule of thumb when you have to make substitutions.

Strawberry Lemonade Splash

Strawberry lemonade is one of summer's most delicious drinks, so why not add a little bit of booze to the party? The Strawberry Lemonade Splash is a very basic strawberry lemonade recipe, with just enough rum to let you know it's there. Whether you're sharing with friends or just relaxing by yourself, this is sure to be a refreshing treat.

4 fresh strawberries (hulled)

½ lemon (juiced)

1 tsp sugar

2 oz rum

6 oz water

1 kiwi circle (garnish)

1 Add the strawberries, lemon juice, and sugar to a blender and blend until smooth.

2 Add ice to two Mason jars, then add the rum and strawberry-lemon puree. Top off with the water and stir until thoroughly mixed.

3 Garnish with a kiwi circle and enjoy!

Fresh fruit is obviously preferable, but you can always use frozen fruit. You can even use repackaged juices if you need to. It won't have the same natural flavor, but it's an effective mixer for rum nevertheless.

Sunburst

Regular rum is delicious, but coconut rum takes things to a whole new level. In fact, among all of rum's flavor variations, coconut is probably the most popular. Unlike most flavored liquors, coconut rum tends to be extremely smooth—almost anyone will find it drinkable. Mix it with a few different tropical flavors, and you're liable to forget you're even drinking!

1 part coconut rum

1 part pineapple juice

2 parts grapefruit juice

1 grapefruit twist (garnish)

1 Add your desired amount of ice to your Mason jar and add the coconut rum, pineapple juice, and grapefruit juice. Stir until thoroughly mixed.

2 Garnish with a grapefruit twist and enjoy!

Try messing around with the ingredient amounts. Coconut rum is so easy to drink that you should feel free to bump up the alcohol content if you're comfortable mixing yourself a stronger drink.

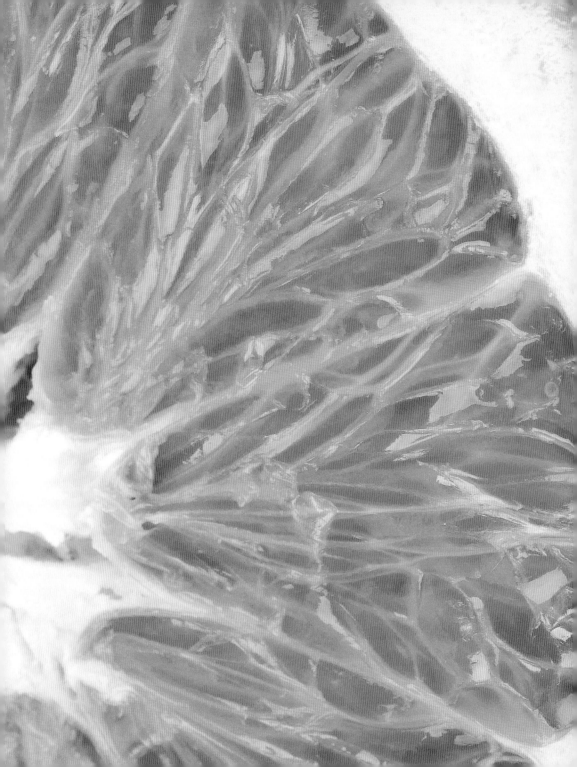

Tropical Spiced Rum

Regular rum, coconut rum, fruity rum...what about spiced rum? There's no reason rum should lose its tropical feel just because there's a little bit of added spice. Tropical Spiced Rum will mentally transport you to a sunny beach just as effectively as any other rum drink—maybe more. Combined with the familiar mixture of orange and pineapple juices, the complexity of flavor added by the rum's spices gives this one a little something extra.

1 part spiced rum

1 part orange juice

1 part pineapple juice

1 splash orange liqueur

1 orange slice (garnish)

1 Fill your Mason jar with ice and add the spiced rum, orange juice, and pineapple juice in approximately equal parts.

2 Top off with a splash of orange liqueur.

3 Garnish with a simple orange slice and enjoy!

Mason Jar Hurricane

One of most frequently ordered drinks on New Orleans's legendary Bourbon Street, the Hurricane is a great little Cajun cocktail that you certainly don't need to be an expert to make. The Hurricane is pretty straightforward, consisting mainly of rum and orange juice, with a dash of passion fruit flavor to give your tongue a little taste of something different. You probably don't have passion fruit syrup lying around at home, but once you've tasted your first Hurricane, you might make a point to grab some. Personalize this one with a splash of pomegranate juice to add a bit of extra depth to the drink!

1 part dark rum

1 part light rum

1 part passion fruit syrup

1 part orange juice

1 splash pomegranate juice

½ lime (juiced)

1 orange wheel (garnish)

1 maraschino cherry (garnish)

1 Add the ingredients (except the orange wheel and maraschino cherry) to a cocktail shaker filled with ice. Shake vigorously.

2 Add ice to your Mason jar and strain the cocktail shaker into it.

3 Garnish with an orange wheel and maraschino cherry and enjoy!

VARIATION

The Hurricane shares its name with a coffee-flavored shooter. You won't want to make one Mason jar–sized, but if you feel like trying this impostor, combine coffee liqueur, orange liqueur, Irish cream, and rum and throw it back!

Banana Cream Pie

Who doesn't love a little bananas and cream? The Banana Cream Pie takes that flavor combo and runs with it. This cocktail doesn't quite achieve smoothie consistency, but neither is it watery.

1 banana (pureed)

1 part vanilla rum

1 part banana rum

1 part cream

Dusting of nutmeg (garnish)

1 banana circle (garnish)

1 Cut a banana circle (peel on) to put aside for a garnish, peel the rest of the banana, and put it in the blender. Blend until smooth.

2 Add the blended banana, rums, and cream to a cocktail shaker filled with ice and shake vigorously. This will take some time to mix completely, so don't let up!

3 Pour the resulting mixture into your Mason jar, adding ice as desired. Top with a dusting of nutmeg and garnish with the banana circle. Enjoy!

VARIATIONS

+ You can alter the consistency as you see fit: add a bit more banana puree for a thicker drink, and add more cream for something a little more sippable.

+ If you *really* love bananas, you might consider including a whole one as a garnish. Peel a banana and cut it in half. Dust it with a bit of cinnamon and crust it with some crushed graham crackers for a delicious and unconventional garnish!

Mason Jar Tom and Jerry

If you like eggnog, you'll love the Tom and Jerry. It's a warm winter cocktail, so you'll want to make sure your Mason jar has a handle (or a coozie!) to avoid burning your hand. It's a pretty boozy concoction, with two full ounces of liquor per serving, but you'd never know it by taste. Topped with warm milk, the Tom and Jerry is the perfect drink to sip on a quiet winter night as you watch the snowflakes fall. Use a cinnamon stick as a stirrer.

1 egg

2 oz simple syrup (page 190)

2 oz dark rum

2 oz brandy

4 oz warm milk

2 cinnamon sticks (garnish)

1 Separate the egg yolk from the egg white and beat them both before recombining into two Mason jars.

2 Add the simple syrup, dark rum, and brandy, then top off each drink with the warm milk.

3 Stir thoroughly and garnish each drink with a cinnamon stick. Enjoy!

VARIATIONS

+ If you're looking to make a large batch of Tom and Jerrys to serve at a party, you should only make the batter. Let guests serve themselves and top off their own drink with warm milk. This will allow them to make the drink as strong or weak as they like, and it will also prevent the ingredients from separating in your punch bowl.

+ The Tom and Jerry is very similar to eggnog. If you're feeling lazy, you could try replacing the egg and simple syrup with a bit of warm eggnog. Be forewarned, though: it isn't going to taste the same.

Spiced Cream

Here's something you probably never thought you'd see: a cocktail made from milk and spiced rum. Well, if you're willing to give this unusual combination a shot, you might find you've got a new favorite. If you're having a few people over and you want to show off your mixology skills, what better to serve them than a drink that will blow all of their preconceptions out of the water? It's a smaller drink, so make sure you're not serving it in a giant, 16-oz jar. This little cocktail packs a major flavor punch.

2 oz spiced rum

1 oz Irish cream

1 tsp sugar

4 oz milk

2 drops vanilla extract

1 drop almond extract

Dusting of nutmeg (garnish)

1 cinnamon stick (garnish)

1 Fill a cocktail shaker with ice and add the ingredients together (except the nutmeg and cinnamon stick for garnish). Shake vigorously until everything is thoroughly mixed.

2 No ice for this one: strain the cocktail shaker into your Mason jar.

3 Hit the top with a little dusting of nutmeg and add a cinnamon stick for garnish. Enjoy!

VARIATION

You can make this cocktail in larger serving sizes by following the 2 parts rum, 1 part Irish cream, 4 parts milk model...but it is not recommended. Milk and rum are an unusual flavor combination, and when the quantities increase, the odds of properly balanced flavors decrease.

Hot Buttered Rum

Hot buttered anything is probably going to sound pretty appetizing, and adding a little rum to the equation provides an unexpected (but welcome) boozy kick to an already delicious drink. Hot Buttered Rum is sort of like tea...without the tea. It's a warm, spicy mixture, with a bit of added creaminess from the butter. You can play with a variety of different spices to personalize the drink, though the most common tend to be cinnamon, nutmeg, and allspice.

1 small pat of butter

1 tsp brown sugar

1 dash cinnamon

1 dash nutmeg

1 dash orange zest

1 small splash vanilla extract

6 oz hot water

2 oz dark rum

1 dash spice (cinnamon, nutmeg, or allspice)

1 cinnamon stick (garnish)

1 Muddle the butter, brown sugar, cinnamon, nutmeg, and orange zest in the bottom of your Mason jar to create a spiced butter mixture. Make sure the ingredients are thoroughly mixed, then add the vanilla extract.

2 Put the kettle on and boil the water like you would for tea.

3 Add the dark rum and hot water to the jar. Add a dash of spice if you'd like (cinnamon, nutmeg, and allspice are typical choices). Mix thoroughly, garnish with a cinnamon stick, and enjoy! This is a hot beverage, so be very careful not to burn your hands.

VARIATIONS

+ Some variations include allspice, while others forego the vanilla extract and orange zest. It's simply a matter of how complex you want the flavor of the drink to be. If you're happy with simply butter and cinnamon, then by all means go for it!

+ Some prefer to make the spiced butter mixture in large batches and refrigerate it for later. This will allow you to easily make Hot Buttered Rum at a moment's notice, rather than having to mix butter and spices for every drink. Hold off on the vanilla extract, and you'll be ready to go in either of two ways: Hot Buttered Rum or Virgin Hot Buttered Rum (page 96).

Virgin Hot Buttered Rum

Yes, throwing "virgin" and "rum" in the name of a cocktail seems like a bit of an oxymoron. But Hot Buttered Rum is such a well-known and delicious beverage that it only seems right to make sure the nonalcoholic version pays the original an appropriate level of homage. It's time to get a little more creative with this one. Since rum isn't available as an ingredient, you'll have to replace the dominant flavor with something even better: ice cream.

1 small pat of butter

1 tsp brown sugar

1 dash cinnamon

1 dash nutmeg

1 dash orange zest

2 oz vanilla ice cream

Hot water to fill

Additional spices as desired

1 cinnamon stick (garnish)

1 Muddle the butter, brown sugar, cinnamon, nutmeg, and orange zest in the bottom of your Mason jar to create a spiced butter mixture. Make sure the ingredients are thoroughly mixed.

2 Put the kettle on and boil some water like you would for tea.

3 Add the vanilla ice cream to the jar and mix it in with the spiced butter. Don't worry about melting—you're about to add the hot water anyway.

4 Fill the remainder of the jar with hot water and stir thoroughly. Add the additional spices as desired and garnish with a cinnamon stick. Enjoy, and don't burn your hands!

As with regular Hot Buttered Rum, feel free to experiment with spices. If the vanilla ice cream isn't providing enough flavor for you, you can also add the small splash of vanilla extract that the original recipe calls for.

MAKES 1 SERVING.

Caribbean Cranberry

Cranberry juice might be the single most essential cocktail ingredient to keep around. It's so useful! So versatile! And it goes with just about every type of alcohol. Whether it's a Vodka Cranberry, Gin and Juice, or, yes, even one of a dozen rum drinks, cranberry juice is the old reliable of the cocktail world. The Caribbean Cranberry brings cranberry juice into the fold in a very familiar way, with a unique twist of coconut rum to keep things fresh.

1 part coconut rum

1 part orange juice

1 part cranberry juice

1 orange slice (garnish)

1 Fill your Mason jar with ice as desired, then add the coconut rum and both juices, and stir until thoroughly mixed.

2 Garnish with an orange slice and enjoy!

CROWD-PLEASER

It's easy to make a big batch of the Caribbean Cranberry—just keep adding the ingredients in equal measure! A bottle of each ingredient should do just fine to fill your bowl with a delicious drink that will keep your guests coming back for more.

Cherry Limeade

Cherry and lime go together about as well as any two flavors on the planet, so why not introduce a little rum to the equation? Cherry Limeade may not have the tropical flair of the pineapple- and coconut–based rum drinks, but it's no less delicious. The perfect cooling refresher, a jar of Cherry Limeade will go a long way on a hot summer day. The grenadine in the drink may seem somewhat superfluous, but in a world where presentation is everything, you'll appreciate not only the subtle flavor but also the bright red color it brings the drink.

1 lime (juiced)

1 tbsp sugar

6 oz water

1 oz grenadine

2 oz cherry rum

1 maraschino cherry (garnish)

1 lime circle (garnish)

1 Juice one full lime into your Mason jar and discard the shell. Add the sugar and water, then stir until the sugar has been dissolved.

2 Add the grenadine and cherry rum, then stir until thoroughly mixed (it should be a rich, red color).

3 Garnish with a maraschino cherry and a lime circle and enjoy!

If you have a favorite recipe for making your own limeade (or even cherry limeade), feel free to use that and simply add in cherry rum!

Virgin Cherry Limeade

As much as everyone loves lemonade as the classic drink of summer, it can get old after your 200th glass of the season. Fortunately, there are plenty of other refreshing flavor combos out there, and cherry and lime makes for one of the best. Who needs booze when you can swap it out for something this flavorful?

1 lime (juiced)

1 tbsp sugar

8 oz water

2 oz grenadine

1 maraschino cherry (garnish)

1 lime circle (garnish)

1 Juice one full lime into your Mason jar and discard the shell. Add the sugar and water, then stir until the sugar has been dissolved.

2 Add the grenadine, then stir until thoroughly mixed (it should be a rich, red color).

3 Garnish with a maraschino cherry and a lime circle and enjoy!

VARIATION

There are obviously hundreds of different recipes out there, depending on whom you ask. If you want to add a bit of extra cherry flavor and you don't mind a little cloying sweetness, try adding a small amount of maraschino cherry juice to the recipe. This will also give it an even brighter red coloration.

Cidermeister

What's better on a cool fall day than some nice, crisp apple cider? There are plenty of cocktails that call for hot apple cider, but what if that's not what you want? Hot apple pie is good, but sometimes you just want some applesauce. The Cidermeister drink balances a handful of flavors that you might not expect to go well together, but hey...who says coconut rum is only good in tropical drinks?

1 part coconut rum

1 part Jagermeister

4 parts fresh apple cider

1 or 2 cinnamon sticks (garnish)

1 Add ice to your Mason jar as desired, and pour in the coconut rum and Jagermeister.

2 Top with fresh apple cider and stir thoroughly.

3 Garnish with a cinnamon stick or two and enjoy!

This cocktail works with regular rum (or even spiced rum) as well, but the coconut rum gives the drink a little extra sweetness and an unusual flavor that makes it unique.

Rum Rum Rudolph

Rum is often used in bright, tropical cocktails, but the Rum Rum Rudolph proves that it can be a fantastic base for wintery drinks as well. It's a sweet cocktail, with the rum mingling nicely with the horchata and the peppermint schnapps adding a refreshing, minty element. It's a drink meant for sipping in front of the fire as the sun gets low, tailor-made for sharing with friends and family while huddled beneath a warm, cozy blanket.

1 oz white rum

1 oz peppermint schnapps

4 oz horchata

1 small candy cane (garnish)

1 Fill your Mason jar approximately halfway with ice, then add the white rum, peppermint schnapps, and horchata. Stir until thoroughly combined.

2 Garnish with a small candy cane and enjoy!

Privateer

This cocktail takes the simplest of ingredients and adds them up to create something considerably greater than the sum of its parts. It's a quick and easy cocktail to make for a crowd, as long as you have a healthy supply of limes!

½ lime (juiced)

1 part coconut rum

3 parts cola

1 lime circle (garnish)

1 Slice one half of a lime into wedges. Squeeze the juice into your Mason jar, then drop the squeezed wedges into the jar.

2 Add ice as desired, then add the coconut rum and cola. Stir until thoroughly mixed.

3 Garnish with a lime circle and enjoy!

VARIATION

Use lemon instead of lime.

Virgin Privateer

With just a tiny modicum of effort, you can add new and exciting flavors to what would otherwise be a simple cola drink!

½ lime (juiced)

1 oz coconut syrup

8 oz cola

1 lemon circle (garnish)

1 Slice one half of a lime into wedges. Squeeze the juice into your Mason jar, then drop the squeezed wedges into the jar.

2 Add ice as desired, then add the coconut syrup and cola. Stir until thoroughly mixed.

3 Garnish with a lime circle and enjoy!

Rum and Coconut

Coconut rum is popular. That should be extremely clear by now. So why not go all out with it? If you're a fan of coconut, the Rum and Coconut is about as coconutty as it gets. Best of all, coconut water is one of the most popular hangover cures out there, which means this drink might actually prevent the very hangover you fear.

1 lemon wedge (garnish)

Toasted coconut shavings (for rimming)

1 part coconut rum

3 parts coconut water

1 Rim the edge of your Mason jar by rubbing the lemon wedge along the rim of the jar and dipping it into a pile of toasted coconut shavings.

2 Add ice as desired to the jar, then add the coconut rum and coconut water. Stir until thoroughly mixed.

3 Stick the original lemon wedge back onto the rim of the jar to garnish and enjoy!

Rimming a glass is a simple process often done for both flavoring and decorative purposes. While sugar and salt are the most common accents, there are many cocktail recipes that call for glasses rimmed with anything from cocoa powder to cayenne pepper. Here, we class up the Rum and Coconut with coconut shavings.

Island Splash

Rum and coconut go together extremely well, and the Island Splash adds peaches and cream to the equation to create a delicious mix of tropical flavors. The coconut cream adds some needed richness to this blended cocktail, which makes the perfect treat for any small gathering of friends or family. You don't have to travel to a tropical island to enjoy this cocktail: one sip will make you feel like you're there.

1 cup coconut rum

1 cup peach rum

¼ cup coconut cream

2 or 3 peaches (pitted and sliced)

4 cups ice (approximately 1 per serving)

Fresh peach slices (garnish)

1 Add the rums, coconut cream, peaches, and ice to a blender and blend to your desired level of smoothness. Add ice as desired until reaching your preferred consistency.

2 Pour into four Mason jars and garnish with fresh peach slices. Enjoy!

Virgin Island Splash Ⓥ

Maybe you don't like rum, or maybe you don't feel like a cocktail. Not to worry: the Virgin Island Splash packs all the flavor of the Island Splash into an alcohol-free alternative. Peaches and cream remain the focal point of this mocktail, with the addition of peach nectar bringing the layer of sweetness provided by the coconut rum in the original. This cocktail can be made in large batches and makes a perfect party drink!

1 cup coconut milk

1 cup peach nectar

2 or 3 peaches (pitted and sliced)

4 cups ice (approximately 1 per serving)

Fresh peach slices (garnish)

1 Add the coconut milk, peach nectar, peaches, and ice to a blender and blend to your desired level of smoothness. Add ice as desired until reaching your preferred consistency.

2 Pour into four Mason jars and garnish with fresh peach slices. Enjoy!

VARIATION

Add a scoop of vanilla ice cream to the blender for added richness!

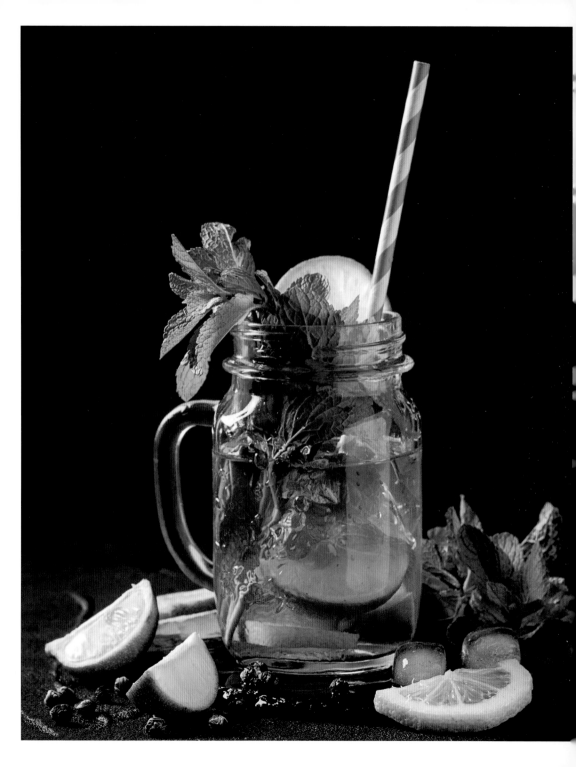

Green Tea Mojito

The Mojito is a popular cocktail, but not everyone loves the aggressive flavor of rum. The Green Tea Mojito helps address this issue by replacing some of the club soda with green tea for a more mellow flavor profile. The herbal nature of green tea works well with the traditionally minty cocktail, creating a Mojito alternative that just about anyone can get on board with.

1 tbsp sugar

½ lime (juiced)

1 cup crushed ice

10 mint leaves

2 oz white rum

4 oz green tea

1 splash club soda

3 or 6 mint sprigs (garnish)

2 lime wheels (garnish)

1 Add the sugar and fresh lime juice to your Mason jar and stir until the sugar is dissolved.

2 Add ¼ of the crushed ice, then take the mint leaves, rub them over the edge of the jar, tear each one in half, and add them on top of the ice. Stir again.

3 Add the white rum, green tea, and the remaining ice. Stir one last time.

4 Top with a splash of club soda, then add mint sprigs and lime wheels for garnish. Enjoy!

VARIATION

While you don't need the splash of club soda, the Mojito is traditionally a fizzy cocktail. However, for a flatter, mellower cocktail, omit the club soda and simply enjoy the green tea.

Bee Aggressive

A play on the traditional Honey Bee cocktail, Bee Aggressive mingles the rich flavor of dark rum with the sweetness of honey, yielding delicious results. This variation incorporates a dash of maple syrup alongside the honey, giving the cocktail an interesting new twist without sacrificing its inherent sweetness. Bee Aggressive lives up to its name: it is both aggressively sweet and aggressively strong, but it's sure to become a favorite among those with a particularly sweet tooth.

½ oz honey

½ oz maple syrup

1 oz warm water

½ oz lemon juice

2 oz dark rum

1 lemon twist (garnish)

1 Stir together the honey, maple syrup, and water in a glass until the honey and syrup dissolve.

2 Add the lemon juice and dark rum to a cocktail shaker filled with ice. Add the honey-and-syrup mixture and shake vigorously.

3 Fill your Mason jar approximately halfway with ice. Strain the mixture from the cocktail shaker into it.

4 Garnish with a lemon twist and enjoy!

TEQUILA-BASED COCKTAILS

Ah, tequila. Ever the Jekyll and Hyde of the alcohol world. Beloved by many and feared by all, tequila's formidable reputation for felling even the most seasoned of drinkers is perhaps only surpassed by its reputation for creating some of the most delicious drinks around. It's no mistake that the Margarita is popular in Mexico, Canada, and everywhere in between. Despite having a strong flavor of its own, tequila's ability to fade into the background allows accents like orange and lime to take the wheel.

Celebrating Cinco de Mayo has become nearly as expected as celebrating the Fourth of July, and no liquor has benefited more greatly from the holiday's rise to prominence than tequila. If you're throwing a party of your own (and you should!), be sure to familiarize yourself with some of the more popular tequila drinks. In the following pages, you'll see not just the Margarita and its many variations, but lesser-known tequila drinks such as the Paloma and Toronha. Delicious in their own right, these drinks might make you forget all about the Margarita and come back for seconds.

Mason Jar Margarita

How could any self-respecting cocktail book omit the beloved Margarita, ever the most popular tequila cocktail? The ability to make a top-shelf Marg' will make you the center of any social event. No need to wait for Cinco de Mayo to break this one out—Margaritas are perfect for sipping at any time of year. Who needs Margarita glasses, anyway?

Salt (for rimming)

3 parts tequila

2 parts orange liqueur

1 part lime juice

1 orange slice (garnish)

1 Rim the edge of your Mason jar with the salt.

2 Fill a cocktail shaker with ice and add your liquid ingredients. Shake well.

3 Add ice to your Mason jar and strain in the tequila mixture. Garnish with a slice of orange and enjoy!

Virgin Margarita

It's hard to replicate the delicious taste of a Margarita, but the Virgin Margarita presents something a little unique. If you're able to accept that this is a different cocktail altogether, you'll almost certainly find yourself enjoying this fresh and fruity concoction. Best made with fresh lemon, lime, and orange juice, the Virgin Margarita is the perfect mocktail for morning, afternoon, or night.

Salt (for rimming)

1 part lemon juice

1 part lime juice

1 part orange juice

1 part simple syrup (page 190)

1 orange wedge (garnish)

1 Rub an orange wedge along the rim of your Mason jar and rim it with the salt.

2 Add the lemon juice, lime juice, orange juice, and simple syrup to a cocktail shaker filled with ice and shake until combined.

3 Add ice to your Mason jar and strain the shaker into it. Garnish with an orange wedge and enjoy!

VARIATION

Virgin Frozen Margarita: Add about a cup of ice (give or take, depending on how thick you want it to be) and blend.

Frozen Margarita

No cocktail book would be complete without the Margarita's possibly even more popular cousin, the Frozen Margarita. Really, why casually sip a tequila drink when you can slurp it down like a slushy? If the regular Mason Jar Margarita just isn't quite cooling you down enough, add some ice to the equation and let this frosty cold treat run wild across your taste buds.

Salt (for rimming)

3 parts tequila

2 parts orange liqueur

1 part lime juice

1 cup ice

1 orange slice (garnish)

1 Rim the edge of your Mason jar with the salt.

2 Add the tequila, orange liqueur, and lime juice to a blender, with about a cup of ice. Add or subtract ice, depending on how thick you like your frozen drinks.

3 Strain the frozen tequila mixture into your Mason jar and garnish with a slice of orange. Enjoy!

To make any flavor of margarita into a frozen drink, just blend with ice (about one cup per serving should do).

Apple Pie Margarita

The Apple Pie Margarita is everything you love about Mom's apple pie, with a warming twist of tequila. You might not have time to whip up a whole apple pie for your party guests, but you can offer them something just as tasty with this original autumn offering.

Cinnamon sugar (for rimming)

2 parts cinnamon tequila

1 part orange liqueur

2 parts apple cider

1 apple slice (garnish)

1 Rim the edge of your Mason jar with the cinnamon sugar.

2 Fill a cocktail shaker with ice and add your liquid ingredients. Shake well.

3 Add ice to your Mason jar and strain in the cinnamon tequila mixture. Garnish with a slice of apple and enjoy!

Raspberry Margarita

Why limit yourself to regular old Margaritas, when there are literally hundreds of different flavor combinations to try out? The Raspberry Margarita doesn't eliminate the lime of the original but plays off it with the simple addition of raspberry liqueur. Raspberry and lime are a natural and timeless combination that you're sure to love.

Salt (for rimming)

3 parts tequila

2 parts orange liqueur

1 part raspberry liqueur

1 part lime juice

1 small handful raspberries (garnish)

1 Rim the edge of your Mason jar with the salt.

2 Fill a cocktail shaker with ice and add your liquid ingredients. Shake well.

3 Add ice to your Mason jar and strain in the tequila mixture. Garnish with a few raspberries and enjoy!

The most commonly recommended liqueur for the Raspberry Margarita is Chambord, which is both awesomely named and awesomely bottled. Supposedly dating back to the 17th century, it's a unique and flavorful raspberry liqueur that you can't go wrong with.

Cranberry Margarita

Give your favorite Margarita recipe a holiday feel with this cranberry variant. As always, cranberry and lime go together extremely well, making this a logical flavor leap for the ever-popular Margarita. Using cranberry juice will give the cocktail a deep, rich color that's beautiful to look at. Throw in a handful of cranberries and a lime wheel for garnish, and you'll be showcasing a red-and-green masterpiece that's a feast for the eyes!

Salt (for rimming)

1 part lime juice

2 parts tequila

1 part orange liqueur

2 parts cranberry juice

1 lime wheel (garnish)

1 handful cranberries (garnish)

1 Rim the edge of your Mason jar with the salt, using the lime juice as a binding agent.

2 Fill a cocktail shaker with ice and add your liquid ingredients. Shake well.

3 Add ice to your Mason jar and strain in the tequila mixture. Garnish with a lime wheel and a handful of cranberries and enjoy!

MAKES 1 SERVING.

Creamsicle Margarita

Rum isn't the only liquor that can get in on the coconut fun; tequila can match up perfectly fine with the flavor. Vanilla and orange might not be the first flavors you would expect to find in a margarita, but if you want to serve something interesting and impress people with a drink they've never seen before, you won't do much better than the Creamsicle Margarita.

Sugar (for rimming)

1 part orange juice

3 parts silver tequila

1 part orange liqueur

1 part vanilla vodka

1 orange wheel (garnish)

1 Rim the edge of your Mason jar with the sugar, using the orange juice as the binding agent.

2 Fill a cocktail shaker with ice and add your liquid ingredients. Shake vigorously until thoroughly mixed.

3 Add ice to your Mason jar and strain in the tequila mixture. Garnish with an orange wheel and enjoy!

Tequila Tropic

Don't limit yourself to vodka and rum when it comes to fruit juices—tequila may have a strong flavor of its own, but citrus fruit can hold its own against just about anything. The Tequila Tropic offers a fun sweet-and-sour mix of citrus flavor to balance out your favorite tequila. It's a summery drink perfect for picnics or backyard gatherings.

1 tsp sugar

4 oz orange juice

½ lemon (juiced)

½ lime (juiced)

2 oz silver tequila

1 orange wheel (garnish)

1 Add the sugar, citrus juices, and silver tequila to a cocktail shaker filled with ice. Shake until thoroughly mixed.

2 Fill your Mason jar halfway with ice and strain the mixture into it. Garnish with an orange wheel and enjoy!

Tequila Sunrise

All right, all right—no more Margaritas. First created around 1930, the Tequila Sunrise is a classic cocktail that has seen countless updates and variations through the years, and is so named because of the way the colorful ingredients seemingly mimic a sunrise. The modern Tequila Sunrise recipe is credited to bartenders Bobby Lazoff and Billy Rice. For the Mason jar version, try spicing it up with a little splash of lime juice.

3 parts tequila

6 parts orange juice

1 part grenadine

1 splash lime juice

1 orange slice (garnish)

1 Pour the tequila and orange juice into your Mason jar.

2 Pour the grenadine into your Mason jar, using a spoon to guide it to the bottom without mixing.

3 Add a splash of lime juice. Garnish with an orange slice and enjoy!

VARIATIONS

+ **Tequila Sunset:** Substitute dark rum or blackberry brandy for the grenadine.

+ **Vodka Sunrise:** Substitute vodka for tequila.

+ **Amaretto Sunrise:** Substitute Amaretto for tequila.

+ **Caribbean Sunrise:** Substitute rum for tequila.

+ **Florida Sunrise:** Made with 3 parts orange juice and 3 parts pineapple juice.

Virgin Sunrise

Drinks like the Vodka Sunrise and the Tequila Sunrise are popular less because they taste delicious (though they certainly do) and more because they look beautiful in the glass. Well, good news: it turns out it's incredibly easy to recreate the visual effect in mocktail form. No liquor necessary for this one—just a simple ingredients featuring all the hues of a morning sunrise.

8 oz orange juice

1 oz grenadine

1 splash lime juice

1 orange slice (garnish)

1 Fill your Mason jar just over halfway with orange juice.

2 Slowly add the grenadine, using a spoon to guide it to the bottom without mixing. Do not stir.

3 Top with the splash of lime juice and add ice as desired. Garnish with an orange slice and enjoy!

VARIATION

Maraschino cherries also make an ideal garnish for the Virgin Sunrise, though it is best to let them sit atop the ice or on the rim of the jar. Otherwise, there is a risk that they may sink to the bottom and disrupt the color of the drink.

El Diablo

One of the most underrated tequila cocktails around, the El Diablo is spicy and fruity all at once. If you love tequila but Margaritas aren't your thing, try this one on for size. With hints of lime and black currant, the El Diablo produces an unfamiliar flavor combination that will dance a sweet jig across your palate. For a boozy fruit-salad garnish, toss in a few raspberries and blackberries.

1½ oz silver tequila

1 oz black-currant liqueur

1 lime (juiced)

Ginger beer to fill

1 lime slice (garnish)

A few blackberries and raspberries (garnish)

1 Fill a cocktail shaker with ice and add the silver tequila, black-currant liqueur, and lime juice. Shake well.

2 Add ice to your Mason jar as desired and strain the mixture into it. Add the ginger beer to fill.

3 Garnish with a slice of lime and drop in a handful of blackberries and raspberries. Enjoy!

VARIATION

Blue Diablo: Substitute blue curaçao for the blackcurrant liqueur and add a splash of lemon juice to lighten the flavor.

Ginger beer has a harsher taste than most carbonated beverages, making it a challenging cocktail component. Unlike club soda or even ginger ale, ginger beer runs the risk of overpowering the flavor of anything you add to it. If you're looking to create some unique cocktails for yourself, make sure your other ingredients are assertive enough to stand out against the ginger beer before you use it. Or just substitute ginger ale.

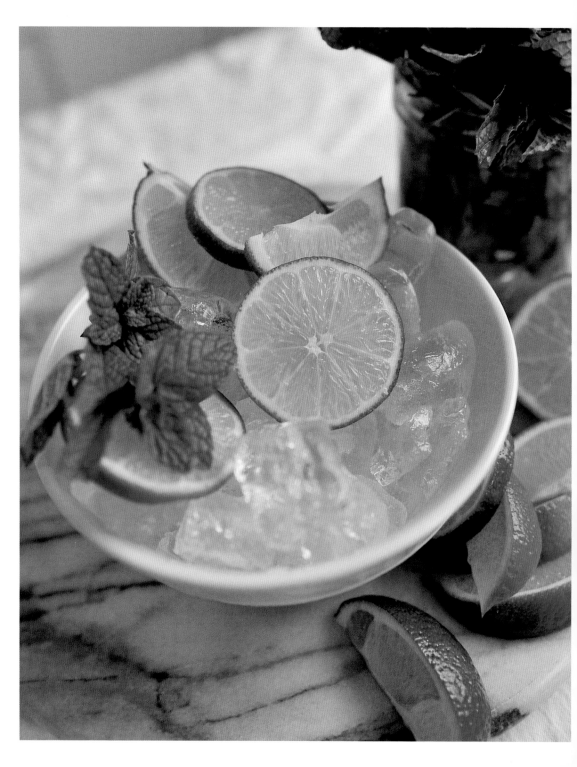

Pepino

Popular among tequila lovers, the Pepino is an underappreciated drink whose fruity bite is tempered only slightly by its tequila base. With pineapple, orange, and lime competing for attention in this medley of flavors, this cocktail will not leave your taste buds wanting. While not typically served with ice, it will take a slightly larger Pepino batch than usual to fill up a Mason jar, and you don't want it getting warm on you!

1 oz simple syrup (page 190)

3 cilantro leaves

3 slices cucumber

2 oz silver tequila

1 oz orange liqueur

1 oz pineapple juice

½ lime (juiced)

1 lime wedge (garnish)

1 pineapple slice
(optional garnish)

1 Add the simple syrup to a cocktail shaker and muddle the cilantro and cucumber slices inside.

2 Add the rest of the liquid ingredients, along with some ice. Shake until thoroughly mixed.

3 Along with your desired amount of ice, strain the mixture into your Mason jar. Drop in a lime wedge or perhaps even a pineapple slice, and enjoy!

Some variations call for the inclusion of egg whites, which you should only do if you feel comfortable with the risks of including raw egg. Most other variations are cosmetic, such as the addition of a dash of agave nectar.

Mason Jar Paloma

About as straightforward as cocktails get, the Paloma is essentially tequila's answer to the Vodka Screwdriver. With a slightly more citrusy kick from the grapefruit juice to counteract the strong flavor of the tequila, the Paloma is a simple and delicious way to freshen up your palate. Of course, the higher the quality of the grapefruit soda, the better your cocktail is going to taste. But if you don't feel like springing for the local organic stuff, regular old Fresca or the like will work just fine. Lime is traditionally used as a garnish, but for the Mason jar version, go ahead and add a little squirt into the drink itself too.

1 part tequila

3 parts grapefruit soda

Splash of lime juice

1 lime slice (garnish)

1 No tricks here! Simply fill your Mason jar with as much ice as you prefer, then add the tequila and grapefruit soda.

2 Add the splash of lime juice, garnish with a slice of lime, and enjoy!

VARIATION

If you're not a fan of grapefruit soda, you can replace it with a mixture of grapefruit juice, club soda, and lime juice.

As with many tequila drinks, rimming the glass with salt is always an option for the Paloma.

CROWD-PLEASER

Squeeze a few limes into your punch bowl, then add in as much tequila and grapefruit soda as you want. The joy of the Paloma is its simplicity—and it's that same simplicity that makes it the perfect large-batch drink.

Tequila Hot Chocolate

Cinco de Mayo may be in the spring, and Margaritas may be a summer drink, but that doesn't mean tequila can't offer a little warmth come wintertime. Tequila Hot Chocolate is the perfect way to warm up in front of a fire or by a window, watching the snow fall.

2 tbsp cocoa powder

3 tsp sugar

1½ cups milk

3 oz milk chocolate chips

2 oz tequila

2 or 3 large marshmallows (garnish)

1 cinnamon stick (garnish)

1 Stir the cocoa powder, sugar, and milk together in a saucepan, and add the chocolate chips. Keep on low to medium heat and stir until the chocolate is melted and thoroughly mixed.

2 Remove from heat and add the tequila. Divide into two Mason jars. Be careful not to burn yourself! You'll want a coozie or a jar with a handle for this drink. Pop a few marshmallows and a cinnamon stick into your hot chocolate and enjoy!

Feel free to swap out some or all of the milk chocolate chips for semisweet or even dark chocolate chips if you're partial to one type of chocolate over another. Some people find that using only milk chocolate chips can make them feel like they're drinking a melted candy bar—a bit too sweet.

Fun Down South

Playing off the idea of a rich mole sauce, Fun Down South is a warm, winter cocktail perfect for those cooler days throughout the year. This is another cocktail that may benefit from a Mason jar with a handle to avoid burning your hands, but the result is well worth it. Hot chocolate and Irish cream are plenty good on their own, but the addition of tequila provides an extra jolt that you'll find very welcome as you strive to stay warm.

2 oz tequila

2 oz Irish cream liqueur

4 oz hot chocolate

Whipped cream (garnish)

1 Add the tequila, Irish cream liqueur, and hot chocolate to your Mason jar. Stir thoroughly until combined.

2 Garnish with whipped cream if desired and enjoy!

MAKES 1 SERVING.

Toronha

Why do so many tequila cocktails involve citrus fruit? Well, because tequila mixes shockingly well with all manner of tropical goodies. In the case of the Toronha, it's grapefruit juice stepping up to the plate and knocking it out of the park. For the Mason jar version, let's temper the sharpness of the grapefruit juice by adding just a splash of orange juice to complement the orange liqueur. With its smoothie-like consistency, the Toronha is perfect for relaxing with in the hammock. No need to worry much about spillage here!

2 oz silver tequila

½ oz orange liqueur

2 oz grapefruit juice

1 splash orange juice

1 splash grenadine

1 cup ice

Fruit of choice (garnish)

1 As you might expect from any recipe involving a substantial amount of ice, add the ingredients (except your fruit garnish) to a blender and blend until smooth.

2 Pour the resulting smoothie into your Mason jar and garnish with the fruit of your choice. Anything from lemon slices to watermelon slices is acceptable, so go crazy and enjoy!

Tequila Grapefruit Cocktail

Similar to the popular Paloma, the Tequila Grapefruit Cocktail is a fruity, carbonated delight. With a touch of ginger ale and orange liqueur to lend some balance to the sharp flavor of the grapefruit juice, this tequila cocktail is a bright and refreshing beverage that goes down easy.

1 part gold tequila

1 part ginger ale

2 parts grapefruit juice

1 splash orange liqueur

1 orange wheel (garnish)

1 Add as much ice to your Mason jar as you want, then add the liquid ingredients together. Stir until thoroughly mixed.

2 Garnish your drink with an orange wheel and enjoy!

Tequila Lemonade

Vodka and gin are the obvious liquors to pair with lemonade, but why let them have all the fun? There's more to tequila than Margaritas, and Tequila Lemonade is proof positive. Don't bother with any of those powdered mixes or store-bought bottles—make your own! Filling a Mason jar with homemade lemonade just feels right, and if there's a drop of tequila in there too? Well, that can be our little secret.

2 lemons (juiced)

1 tsp sugar

4 mint leaves

2 oz silver tequila

6 oz water

1 lemon wheel (garnish)

1 Squeeze two lemons' worth of juice into your Mason jar and add the sugar. Stir until the sugar has mostly dissolved. Add your desired amount of ice.

2 Rub one of the mint leaves around the rim of the jar. Tear all of the leaves in half and add them to the jar, on top of the ice.

3 Add the silver tequila, then top off with the water. Stir until completely mixed. Garnish with a lemon wheel and enjoy!

As with all lemonade, if you want it to be sweeter, add more sugar. If you want it to be more sour, add more lemon juice. Reconfigure the proportions until it makes you happy!

MAKES 1 SERVING.

Mexican Mule

A favorite variant of the Moscow Mule, the Mexican Mule takes the same basic concept and substitutes the chief liquor of Mexico: tequila. Interestingly, tequila and ginger beer go together extremely well—arguably better than the original vodka and ginger beer. If you're a fan of the spicy harshness of ginger beer and you love drinking tequila, this is definitely a drink you're going to want to try. As with its vodka-based sister drink, try including a mint sprig as a garnish to add a bit of extra color and brightness.

½ lime (juiced)

1 part tequila

3 parts ginger beer

1 lime wedge (garnish)

1 mint sprig (garnish)

1 Juice one half of a lime into your Mason jar. Add your desired amount of ice.

2 Pour in the tequila and top off with ginger beer. Garnish with a wedge of lime and a mint sprig and enjoy!

VARIATION

Moscow Mule: The Mexican Mule is itself a variation of the original Moscow Mule (page 33), which is made with vodka rather than tequila.

Frozen Tequila Refresher

Lime goes well with just about anything, and watermelon is no exception. The Frozen Tequila Refresher will keep you cool on even the hottest summer days. Made with fresh watermelon and lime, this might be a drink you want to make in larger batches. This recipe is for a single serving, but you can multiply it and prepare a pitcher for everyone.

1 cup watermelon

1 oz simple syrup (page 190)

2 oz silver tequila

½ lime (juiced)

1 cup ice

1 lime wheel (garnish)

1 Remove the seeds from the watermelon.

2 Add the watermelon, simple syrup, silver tequila, and lime juice to a blender, along with the 1 cup of ice. Puree until smoothie-like in consistency.

3 Pour into your Mason jar and garnish with a lime wheel. Enjoy!

Frozen Watermelon Lime Refresher

Just as delicious as the Frozen Tequila Refresher, the Frozen Watermelon Lime Refresher is a fruity slush that everyone can enjoy. Nothing compares to the taste of a fresh watermelon puree with sugar and lime on a burning-hot day. Get the fresh fruit, and do the work. Carve that watermelon. You'll thank yourself later.

3 cups watermelon

2 oz simple syrup (page 190)

2 limes (juiced)

2 cups ice

2 lime wheels (garnish)

1 Remove the seeds from the watermelon.

2 Add the watermelon, simple syrup, and lime juice to a blender, along with the two cups of ice (one per serving). Puree until smoothie-like in consistency.

3 Pour into two Mason jars and garnish each one with a lime wheel. Enjoy!

Mason jars can be a great way to dress up individual servings, but what about if you're making a large batch of something? Punch bowls are so boring and utilitarian. Why not hollow out a watermelon for a unique and whimsical twist on the classic serving bowl? Simply slice a hole in the side and hollow it out, just like you would a pumpkin. You can use the meat of the watermelon to make a drink such as the Watermelon Vodka Refresher (page 14), presented in a fun way that's sure to be a conversation starter!

Apple Tart

This strong drink is a St. Patrick's Day favorite. You won't want to have too many of them, as the drink is almost entirely alcohol, but my goodness, are they delicious. It's hard to go wrong with a combination of schnapps and tequila, and the Apple Tart blends them together brilliantly. Try to choose a brand of schnapps with a bright green color, and you'll have a delicious apple drink with a citrus twist to dazzle your St. Patrick's Day guests.

2 oz tequila

1 oz apple schnapps

1 oz apple juice

1 lime (juiced)

1 lime wheel (garnish)

1 Add the ingredients (except the lime wheel garnish) to a cocktail shaker filled with ice. Shake vigorously.

2 Fill your Mason jar with ice and strain the tequila mixture into it. Garnish with a lime wheel and enjoy!

CROWD-PLEASER

There aren't all that many apple-based cocktails, so the Apple Tart gives you the opportunity to show your guests something a little different. With just a bottle of tequila, a half bottle of apple schnapps, a half bottle of apple juice, and a few limes for flavor, you'll have a gorgeous, colorful, and unusual drink to showcase for your friends and family.

Tequila Sour

The Tequila Sour isn't far removed from the Margarita, and while Margarita variations have been done to death, if you're a fan of the Margarita, you might want to give this one a try. The Tequila Sour is already a bright, vibrant drink, but some fresh blueberries and mint give it a little added flair.

1 lemon (juiced)

2 oz tequila

1 tsp sugar

1 handful blueberries

1 or 2 lemon wheels

1 mint sprig (garnish)

1 Juice the lemon into a cocktail shaker, then add the tequila and sugar. Shake vigorously.

2 Add ice to your Mason jar, along with a handful of blueberries and a lemon wheel or two.

3 Strain the cocktail shaker into it and garnish with a mint sprig. Enjoy!

Virgin Sour

Stripping away the tequila and swapping in a bit of fizzy ginger ale might break convention a bit, but it does produce a bright and flavorful virgin alternative to the Tequila Sour.

1 lemon (juiced)

1 tsp sugar

2 oz ginger ale

1 splash grenadine

1 lemon slice (garnish)

1 maraschino cherry (garnish)

1 Add the lemon juice and sugar to your Mason jar and stir until mostly dissolved. Top off with the ginger ale and stir again.

2 Add the splash of grenadine to give the drink a bit of color. Do not stir. Garnish with a slice of lemon and a maraschino cherry and enjoy!

Mason Jar Bloody Maria

It doesn't take a genius to figure out what the Bloody Maria is: it's a Bloody Mary with tequila. In a way, this makes perfect sense. The best hangover cure is often said to be hair of the dog, so, if you spent last night drinking tequila, shouldn't you be drinking tequila to clear your head? Much like the original Bloody Mary, there are countless Bloody Maria variations. Here's one with an extra bit of Mexican flair.

Cracked black pepper (for rimming)

1 lemon wedge (garnish)

2 oz gold tequila

½ oz olive juice

1 lime wedge (juiced)

2 dashes horseradish

Tomato juice to fill

3 drops Worcestershire sauce

3 dashes hot sauce

1 dash black pepper

2 dashes celery salt

1 celery stick (garnish)

1 Rim the edge of your Mason jar with the cracked black pepper (use the lemon wedge as the binding agent).

2 Add the gold tequila, olive juice, lime juice, and horseradish into your jar, along with a handful of ice cubes. Top with the tomato juice and stir until thoroughly mixed.

3 Add the Worcestershire sauce, hot sauce, pepper, and celery salt. Stir again until mixed.

4 Garnish with a large celery stick and the lemon wedge. Enjoy!

As with the Bloody Mary, there are too many variations to even know where to begin. Once you have a general sense of what you like in a Bloody Maria, you can start to do what every bartender in the world does: experiment with new ingredients until you find something that works for you.

Tropical Squeeze

It's no surprise that pineapple and orange make a winning flavor combination, but the addition of tequila provides a mellow roundness that works shockingly well. With a splash of lime juice adding a bit of tartness on the finish, the balance of flavors in this cocktail will be sure to please just about any palate.

4 oz pineapple juice

2 oz tequila blanco

1 oz orange liqueur

1 splash lime juice

1 pineapple wedge (garnish)

1 Add ice to your Mason jar. Pour in the pineapple juice, tequila blanco, and orange liqueur. Stir until thoroughly combined.

2 Top with a splash of lime juice and garnish with a pineapple wedge. Enjoy!

Teq Savvy

Part of creating a winning cocktail is knowing how to coax the most flavor out of your ingredients without allowing any one of them to become overwhelming. Teq Savvy takes a, well, savvy approach to tequila, balancing it with orange, cherry, and lime while finishing with your bubbly of choice. The result is a drink with a surprising depth of flavor and a refreshing effervescence that will leave you wanting more.

2 oz silver tequila

4 oz orange juice

1 splash cherry liqueur

1 splash lime juice

2 oz champagne or prosecco

Maraschino cherries (garnish)

1 Fill your Mason jar approximately halfway with ice. Add the silver tequila, orange juice, cherry liqueur, and lime juice. Stir thoroughly.

2 Top with the champagne or prosecco. Garnish with maraschino cherries and enjoy!

Gold Medal Game

Have you ever mixed orange juice and cranberry juice? It's a great way to start your morning. Gold Medal Game is an ideal brunch cocktail, perfect for sipping while you wait for football, soccer, or any other sport to start. The understated profile of the tequila makes this a perfect complement to the in-your-face nature of the cranberry juice, and the addition of orange and lime creates a surprisingly complex blend of flavors.

2 oz gold tequila

1 oz orange liqueur

2 oz cranberry juice

2 oz orange juice

1 splash lime juice

1 orange wheel (garnish)

1 Add the gold tequila, orange liqueur, cranberry juice, and orange juice to a cocktail shaker filled with ice. Shake vigorously.

2 Strain the resulting mixture into a Mason jar filled with ice.

3 Top with a splash of lime juice and garnish with an orange wheel. Enjoy!

MAKES 1 SERVING.

Azure

If you're not familiar with blue curaçao, it is an orange-flavored liqueur with one exceptional quality: its bright blue color. As a result, it can be used to create some beautiful color effects in cocktails. Simply replacing triple sec with blue curaçao can turn a boring cocktail into a feast for the eyes. There is no better example of that than the Azure, which takes the core components of a traditional Margarita and adds a colorful twist. As the blue curaçao settles, it becomes a particularly pleasing shade of blue in the lower reaches of the jar.

Salt (for rimming)

3 oz tequila

2 oz blue curaçao

1 oz lime juice

1 orange slice (garnish)

1 Rim the edge of your Mason jar with the salt.

2 Fill a cocktail shaker with ice and add the tequila, blue curaçao, and lime juice. Shake vigorously.

3 Fill your Mason jar approximately halfway with ice and strain in the tequila mixture. Garnish with a slice of orange and enjoy!

VARIATION

Mason Jar Cocktails, Expanded Edition contains no shortage of Margarita variants. Some of them could also benefit from a bit of blue. Experiment and find out!

GIN-BASED COCKTAILS

Some say gin reminds them of summer, while for others it evokes feelings of Christmas. Whichever the case may be for you, this disparity is reflected in the wide variety of cocktails in which gin is represented. From the simple and classic Gin and Tonic to the much more complex Strawberry Gin Mojito, gin is the juniper anchor in an ever-swirling sea of flavors.

Gin and lime is a classic pairing, but gin and lemon works nearly as well. And while you might not predict that gin would pop up in a warm drink, be prepared to have your expectations defied. This is something you can use to your advantage! When hosting a gathering, there is nothing better than being able to show off and give your guests something they haven't tried before. All too often, gin finds itself an afterthought when it comes to cocktails, but you can change that by mixing up a batch of Strawberry Basil Lemonade. Once you taste it, you might not even believe it's gin!

When it comes to dressing up gin cocktails, it's just as easy as vodka. A dash of color can go a long way, and you'll find that even just a bit of grapefruit juice will give gin cocktails a vibrant pop of color and freshness that will make your mouth water.

Tom Collins

Named after a famous hoax from the late 1800s, the Tom Collins is one of the more popular gin drinks around. Originally a variation of the John Collins whiskey drink, the Tom Collins has taken on a life of its own. It's not hard to see why. Using gin provides a much lighter base than whiskey, and its crisp, fresh taste makes it much more accessible to the average drinker. It's a sweet, carbonated treat featuring several different fruit flavors that play off each other deliciously. Though the Tom Collins is traditionally made with just lemon juice, the Mason jar version will benefit from a splash of lime juice as well.

2 parts gin

1 tsp sugar

1 part lemon juice

1 part lime juice

4 parts soda water

1 orange slice (garnish)

1 maraschino cherry (garnish)

1 Add the gin, sugar, and juices to an ice-filled shaker. Shake well.

2 Strain the liquid into your Mason jar and top with the soda water. Stir until completely mixed.

3 Garnish with an orange slice and a maraschino cherry. Enjoy!

VARIATIONS

+ **John Collins:** Substitute bourbon/whiskey for gin.

+ **Sandy Collins:** Substitute Scotch for gin.

+ **Brandy Collins:** Substitute brandy for gin.

+ **Vodka Collins:** Substitute vodka for gin.

+ **Ron Collins:** Substitute rum for gin.

+ **Juan Collins:** Substitute tequila for gin.

Mason Jar Greyhound

Along with its sister cocktail (the less appetizing-sounding "Salty Dog"), the Greyhound is a citrusy drink perfect for cooling down during the dog days of summer (get it?). Eschewing popular citrus drinks such as lemonade in favor of the ever-underappreciated grapefruit juice, the Greyhound cocktail is a sweet-and-sour masterpiece. Give it a personal spin with a unique garnish, such as a grapefruit twist.

1 part gin

2 parts grapefruit juice

1 grapefruit twist (garnish)

1 sprig rosemary (garnish)

1 Fill your Mason jar with ice and pour in the gin.

2 Top with the grapefruit juice and stir.

3 Garnish with a grapefruit twist and a sprig of rosemary. Enjoy!

VARIATIONS

+ There seems to be a fifty-fifty split among mixologists and bartenders about whether the Greyhound ought to be made with gin or vodka. Both are equally acceptable, but the juniper flavor of gin contributes a bit more personality to the drink than vodka is capable of adding.

+ **Salty Dog:** To make your Greyhound into a Salty Dog, simply salt the rim of the Mason jar beforehand.

CROWD-PLEASER

With just a bottle of gin and two bottles of grapefruit juice, you've got the perfect large-batch cocktail for your party. You don't want to forget the garnishes for this one—the rosemary adds a distinct flavor to the drink, and the grapefruit twist gives it a classy feel it might otherwise lack.

Singapore Sling

This well-beloved cocktail creates a medley of different types of alcohol bouncing across your palate. It's a tasty cocktail, but also a strong one—you'll want to be careful about having too many of these. One of the more unusual ingredients is Bénédictine, a French liqueur that can be difficult to find. Bénédictine does have a very distinctive herbal taste, making it difficult to substitute for. But if you are dying to try this Mason jar version of the Singapore Sling and can't find a bottle, the closest flavor approximation is Drambuie. Be a little creative and include a unique medley of fruit garnishes, such as orange wheels and maraschino cherries, to give the drink a fresher, brighter feel!

1 part gin

1 part cherry brandy

1 part Bénédictine

1 part lime juice

2 parts club soda

1 dash bitters

Fruit slices as desired (garnish)

1 Fill a cocktail shaker with ice and add all the liquid ingredients except the club soda and bitters. Shake well.

2 Add ice to your Mason jar, then strain the cocktail shaker into it. Add the club soda and the dash of bitters, then stir it up. Garnish with the fruit slices of your choice and enjoy!

VARIATION

Gin Sling: Made with sweet vermouth instead of Bénédictine, lemon juice instead of lime juice, and no cherry brandy. It's a bit lighter and sweeter, with a touch of simple syrup (page 190) added as well. Garnish this one with a lemon slice.

Variants of the Singapore Sling include grenadine and pineapple juice, but the recipe presented here is the simpler original. Simpler is usually better, don't you think?

MAKES 1 SERVING.

Corpse Reviver

As the name might suggest, the Corpse Reviver is a classic morning cocktail designed to cure those pesky hangovers. It's the perfect Bloody Mary substitute for those who just can't understand how a tomato juice–based cocktail became so popular. The most popular variant in the Corpse Reviver family of cocktails, the Corpse Reviver is a bit heavier on booze than a Mimosa, so you'll want to serve this one in small doses! This is the perfect drink to whip up after a couple of friends have stayed the night. Personalize the drink with a dash of bitters to temper its sweetness.

1 part gin

1 part orange liqueur

1 part lemon juice

1 part white wine

1 dash bitters

1 Add the ingredients together in a cocktail shaker filled with ice. Shake vigorously.

2 Strain the resulting mixture into your Mason jar. No ice for this one; you'll want to drink it neat. Enjoy!

Some variations call for the addition of a splash of absinthe to the drink, but absinthe can be a bit hard to come by in the United States. Its inclusion is primarily to add to the aroma of the drink, so it can be safely ignored.

Mason Jar Gin Fizz

The juniper flavor of gin can be bold and overpowering, so it's often best to keep your gin-based cocktails as simple as possible. It's a liquor that pairs well with citrus flavors (if you've ever ordered a gin and tonic, you know it's never served without a slice of lime), and the Gin Fizz drives this point home by calling for almost as much lemon juice as gin. With a hefty dose of powdered sugar, this is the perfect sweet-and-sour drink to sip on a hot day. Give this Mason jar version a twist by adding a splash of grenadine to lend it a light, rosy color!

1.5 oz gin

1 oz lemon juice

1 tsp powdered sugar

4 oz club soda

1 splash grenadine

1 lemon slice (garnish)

1 Fill a cocktail shaker with ice and add the gin, lemon juice, and powdered sugar. Shake well.

2 Add ice to your Mason jar as desired and strain the mixture into it. Add the club soda to fill and add a splash of grenadine.

3 Garnish with a slice of lemon and enjoy!

VARIATIONS

Most Gin Fizz variants feature the inclusion of raw egg. If you're feeling bold, you can try a **Silver Fizz** (add in one egg white), a **Golden Fizz** (add in one egg yolk), or a **Royal Fizz** (add in one whole egg).

Egg whites are often used to "froth" drinks, but before you run around cracking eggs into your cocktails, you'll want to know how to safely incorporate them. Avoid using any egg that appears damaged, and rinse the eggs before using. Don't use the shell to separate the egg white, though: shells can be a haven for germs, even after cleaning. Frothing the egg can take a little bit of extra effort with the cocktail shaker, but can be well worth it.

MAKES 1 SERVING.

Bright Ruby

Orange, grapefruit, and gin produce a celebrated flavor combination and a sunny and cheerful medley of colors that can add a splash of brightness to any gathering. Sweet and bubbly, the Bright Ruby is a grapefruit juice–based gin cocktail with a gorgeous red color (from which it obviously takes its name). To make that color even richer, you can add a small splash of grenadine as well! Similar to the Greyhound, the Bright Ruby puts a tasty twist on an old classic and is a great way to surprise guests with an unexpected depth of flavor.

1 part gin

1 splash orange liqueur

2 parts grapefruit juice

2 parts club soda

1 splash grenadine

1 orange slice (garnish)

1 Fill a cocktail shaker with ice and add the gin, orange liqueur, and grapefruit juice. Shake until mixed thoroughly.

2 Add ice to your Mason jar and strain in the grapefruit juice mixture. Top with the club soda and add the splash of grenadine. Stir until evenly mixed.

3 Garnish with an orange slice and enjoy!

CROWD-PLEASER

As long as you have a good amount of grapefruit juice and club soda, this is a pretty easy one to mix up in large quantities. Keep the 1:2:2 proportions between the gin, grapefruit juice, and club soda, then add orange liqueur for taste and grenadine for color. You can eyeball the drink and decide what works best for you! Add some orange circles and grapefruit slices to your punch bowl for a dressed-up look.

Gin Rickey

Not a complicated drink, the Gin Rickey isn't much more than gin and club soda with a hint of lime. Although the Rickey is a classic bourbon drink that originally hails from the nation's capital, where it was created by a local bartender and named for a lobbyist, it wasn't until the drink was made with gin that it became famous. It's the perfect gin drink to whip up for a few friends when you want to entertain without too much effort.

1 part gin

½ lime (juiced)

4 parts club soda

1 lime wedge (garnish)

1 Add the gin to your Mason jar, then squeeze the juice from one half of a lime into the jar and drop the remainder in as well. Stir, then add ice.

2 Top the drink off with the club soda and garnish with a lime wedge and maybe even some lime circles. Enjoy!

VARIATION

Garnish with a grapefruit twist instead of lime.

If you're finding the drink a little too bitter for your palate, you can add a tiny bit of sugar to taste.

Lime Rickey

A bit heavier on the lime juice and with a little added sugar to make up for the loss of the gin, the Lime Rickey is a delicious and refreshing virgin variation of one of the most popular drinks in the world.

1 part simple syrup (page 190)

1 lime (juiced)

4 parts club soda

1 lime wedge (garnish)

1 Add the simple syrup to your Mason jar, then squeeze the juice from two lime halves into the jar. Drop one of the halves into the drink and stir, then add ice.

2 Top the drink off with the club soda and garnish with a lime wedge. Enjoy!

VARIATION

Garnish with a grapefruit twist.

If you're looking for a way to add a bit of personality to your Mason jar presentation, forget sipping from the lip—try punching holes in the lids. Go out and get yourself some colorful acrylic straws and bring some extra life to the party! If you're feeling particularly artsy and you have the right tools, you can even carve fun and unique designs.

Mason Jar Gin and Tonic

The Gin and Tonic might be the oldest drink in the book, but that's why they call it a classic. Just as delicious after all these years, the flavor combination of tonic water and juniper just can't go wrong. Still, there's always room for improvement, and the Mason Jar Gin and Tonic introduces a few new flavors that make the drink shine. Serve this drink at a party, and your friends will wonder what your secret is.

2 oz gin

1 small handful rosemary leaves

4 oz tonic water

1 lime wedge (garnish)

1 sprig rosemary (garnish)

1 Add the gin and rosemary leaves to a cocktail shaker filled with ice. Shake well.

2 Strain the rosemary-infused gin into your Mason jar.

3 Pour in the tonic water and garnish with a lime wedge and sprig of rosemary. Enjoy!

VARIATIONS

The Gin and Tonic is an extremely adaptable cocktail that lends itself well to all sorts of flavors. Try replacing the rosemary with blackberry or strawberry, or even a subtle vegetable like cucumber. Experiment and see what you like best!

The Mason Jar Gin and Tonic is itself a variation of the classic Gin and Tonic, which simply omits the rosemary.

MAKES 1 SERVING.

South Side

Named after the South Side of Chicago, where the drink originates, the South Side is a lemony fresh concoction similar in style to a Mojito. Rather than filling you up with rum, the South Side opts for the juniper flavor of gin, creating a minty, lemony mix of spring and winter flavors. It's a neat, crisp-looking cocktail that will impress anyone you hand it to. To give your Mason jar version an added bit of flavor and color, add a splash of limoncello to the mix, if you can get your hands on some.

2 oz gin

1 splash limoncello

2 tsp sugar

1 lemon (juiced)

4 mint leaves

1 lemon slice (garnish)

1 mint sprig (garnish)

1 Add the gin, limoncello, sugar, lemon juice, and mint leaves to a cocktail shaker filled with ice.

2 Shake vigorously (hard enough to bruise the mint leaves and release the flavor) until mixed.

3 Fill your Mason jar with ice, then strain the cocktail shaker into it. Garnish with a slice of lemon and a mint sprig and enjoy!

While serving drinks in Mason jars is a great way to add a fun bit of personality to any occasion, why stop there? Mason jars are the perfect vessel for a wide variety of accent pieces, from flowers to candles! Make your table settings pop with a Mason jar theme that goes beyond cocktails. Pack a jar with fresh fruit for people to nibble on (don't forget the toothpicks!) and light a few candles in Mason jars outside to keep the party going into the night.

MAKES 1 SERVING.

Strawberry Basil Lemonade

Lemonade is refreshing, but a bit boring by itself. Adding gin to the mix will give it a welcome dose of that juniper flavor. Why not add a little fresh fruit to the drink as well? And when it comes to herbs, you'd be surprised what a welcome addition basil can be to many cocktails. This Strawberry Basil Lemonade recipe is a little off the beaten path, but it's the perfect Mason jar cocktail: rustic, creative, and delicious.

1 strawberry (sliced and hulled)

2 basil leaves

2 oz gin

1 splash strawberry vodka

3 oz lemonade

1 splash club soda

1 strawberry (garnish)

1 Muddle the strawberry and basil in the bottom of your Mason jar, then add ice.

2 Pour in the gin, strawberry vodka, and lemonade, then stir until mixed.

3 Top with a splash of club soda for some fizz, and garnish with one whole strawberry. Enjoy!

VARIATION

For bigger strawberry flavor, try blending up a little strawberry puree. Add it to a cocktail shaker with the lemonade and shake it up. This will give you a stronger strawberry taste, not to mention a brighter, more visually arresting cocktail!

Peach Gin Tea

When you think of iced tea cocktails, chances are you think of vodka drinks. Maybe whiskey or rum. But gin? Probably not. It turns out gin is a surprisingly tasty addition to most standard teas, especially when combined with complementary flavors like peach. Peach Gin Tea is the perfect cocktail to whip up in large batches for a party, or even just for keeping around in a pitcher to dip into after a long day at work.

4 oz iced tea

2 oz gin

2 oz peach puree

1 tsp sugar

2 or 3 peach wedges (garnish)

1 Combine the iced tea, gin, peach puree, and sugar in a cocktail shaker filled with ice. Shake until thoroughly mixed.

2 Add ice to your Mason jar, then strain the cocktail shaker into it.

3 Add a few peach wedges as a garnish and enjoy!

With flavor-infused iced teas, it is sometimes better to refrigerate the mixture to let the flavors blend together. If you're making a larger batch, you might want to fill a pitcher or punch bowl and leave it in the fridge for a few hours before stirring it up, adding ice, and serving.

MAKES 1 SERVING.

Gin Christmas

Gin isn't the first liquor you think of when it comes to warm drinks, but in this case, the cranberry and mint combine to create a tea-based beverage that will warm you up on a cold winter night. Spice it up with a candy cane to give it that Christmasy feel. As with all warm drinks, this is one for which you'll want to make sure you use a jar with a handle.

6 oz mint tea (hot)

2 oz gin

1 oz cranberry simple syrup (see sidebar below)

½ lemon (juiced)

1 lemon slice (garnish)

1 peppermint stick (garnish)

1 On the stove, boil some water, then add a mint tea bag. Let sit until the tea is ready.

2 Add the gin, cranberry simple syrup, and lemon juice to your Mason jar and stir together.

3 Strain the hot-water-and-mint mixture into the jar and discard the used tea leaves. Stir again. Garnish with a slice of lemon and a peppermint stick and enjoy!

You'll quickly notice that many cocktails call for **simple syrup**. You could always just add sugar and water to your drinks, but it usually isn't the same. Fortunately, simple syrup is as simple to make as its name suggests. Simply combine water and sugar in a 1:1 ratio and boil! As it boils, you'll see it become increasingly cloudy. Don't worry—by the time you're done, the syrup will be completely clear. That's how you know it's done! For Gin Christmas, dice cranberries and add them to the pot when you boil your sugar and water. The same can be done with other fruits to make flavorful syrups of all kinds.

MAKES 1 SERVING.

Strawberry Gin Mojito

Typically a Mojito is made with rum, but this is a play on the English Mojito variation, which calls for gin. The Strawberry Gin Mojito proves once again that gin can work with just about any fruit flavor, playing strawberry and lime off each other for a mix of flavors you won't soon forget. It's a beautiful, bright-red cocktail that will draw everyone's eye and certainly won't leave them disappointed.

2 strawberries (hulled and sliced)

2 oz gin

½ oz simple syrup (page 190)

½ lime (juiced)

1 oz club soda

1 mint sprig (garnish)

1 Muddle the strawberries in the bottom of your Mason jar. Add ice.

2 Add the gin, simple syrup, and lime juice to a cocktail shaker filled with ice and shake vigorously.

3 Strain the shaker into your Mason jar and stir thoroughly. The juice from the strawberries should create a rich, red color.

4 Top with the club soda and stir again. Garnish with a sprig of mint and enjoy!

VARIATION

If you find yourself wanting a stronger strawberry flavor, add more strawberries to the recipe. Likewise, if you want a stronger red color for presentation's sake, a splash of grenadine would not go awry.

Blueberry Sparkler

As easy as it gets, the Blueberry Sparkler combines fruit, gin, and a little bit of fizz. It's an uncomplicated and delicious take on a simple gin and soda drink, and what little effort it requires to make will be repaid tenfold in taste. Mason jar drinks cry out for simplicity. Serve something too fancy in a repurposed jar, and it just doesn't make sense. The Blueberry Sparkler packs all the flavor of a mixologist's most complex creation with the elegant ease of a gin and tonic.

2 oz gin

1 oz blueberry simple syrup (page 190)

½ lemon (juiced)

1 oz club soda

1 lemon circle (garnish)

1 Combine the gin, blueberry simple syrup, and lemon juice in a cocktail shaker filled with ice and shake vigorously.

2 Add ice to your Mason jar and strain the cocktail shaker into it. Top with the club soda and garnish with a lemon circle. Enjoy!

This is a simple recipe that works with just about any fruit. Just make the appropriate infusion of simple syrup and switch it in. Lemon complements most fruits well, so you shouldn't even have to adjust the rest of the recipe.

Blackberry Punchout

A gin-based punch is a bit of an oddity, but its unusual nature is part of its appeal. Spiking fruit juice with vodka is old hat, but mixing a little gin with some fruit and lemonade is a great way to keep things fresh and new. With just a couple of blackberries and a little bit of mint, you've transformed a simple gin and lemonade drink into something that will really impress.

6 blackberries

4 mint leaves

1 splash simple syrup (page 190)

2 oz gin

3 oz lemonade

1 splash grenadine

1 or 2 blackberries (garnish)

1 Muddle the blackberries and mint in the simple syrup at the bottom of a cocktail shaker, then add ice and the gin, lemonade, and grenadine. Shake vigorously.

2 Strain the resulting mixture into your Mason jar after adding your desired amount of ice. Add a blackberry or two for garnish and enjoy!

VARIATIONS

Try the Punchout with other fruits as well: blueberry, strawberry, and cranberry lend themselves particularly well to this drink.

MAKES 1 SERVING.

Mason Jar Negroni

The Negroni is a classic cocktail, balancing bitter Campari with sweet vermouth against a crisp backdrop of gin. A rich burnt orange in color, this is an instantly recognizable cocktail that wears its class and distinction on its sleeve. While a traditional Negroni is made with equal parts gin, Campari, and sweet vermouth, the Mason jar version pulls back on the sweet vermouth, letting the flavor of the gin sing without fear of being overwhelmed.

2 oz gin

2 oz Campari

1 oz sweet vermouth

1 orange peel (garnish)

1 Add the liquid ingredients to a Mason jar filled with ice. Stir until thoroughly combined.

2 Add a sliver of orange peel for garnish and enjoy!

VARIATIONS

If you're feeling bold, use a match or a lighter to singe the orange peel before adding it as a garnish. This caramelizes some of the oil and sugar in the rind, helping to bring out some additional flavor in the fruit and adding a delicious new layer of complexity to the drink.

The Boulevardier is another popular cocktail that swaps out the gin in favor of whiskey. Give it a try and see which version you like better!

Mason Jar Sling

"Sling" cocktails come in many varieties, but the term traditionally refers to any cocktail made with sweet vermouth, lemon juice, sugar, bitters, club soda, and some form of liquor. The Mason Jar Sling is a version of the most popular variant, the Gin Sling. The drink incorporates these traditional ingredients atop a foundation of gin, creating a sunset-colored cocktail to help you wind down at the end of a long day.

2 oz gin

1 oz sweet vermouth

1 oz simple syrup (page 190) (or 1 sugar cube)

1 splash lemon juice

1 dash bitters

3 oz club soda

1 lemon twist (garnish)

1 Add the gin, sweet vermouth, simple syrup, lemon juice, and bitters to a cocktail shaker filled with ice. Shake vigorously.

2 Add ice to your Mason jar and strain the cocktail shaker into it. Top with the club soda.

3 Add a lemon twist for garnish and enjoy!

VARIATIONS

While gin is the most popular liquor to include in a Sling-style cocktail, you can substitute your liquor of choice. The Whiskey Sling, Rum Sling, and even Tequila Sling are all popular in their own right.

MAKES 1 SERVING.

Botanical Bouquet

Lavender is a uniquely floral flavor, and its aromatic nature has made it one of the most popular gin botanicals. Better still, the delicate beauty and pleasing shade of lavender itself makes it the perfect garnish for a cocktail you'll be proud to show off. If you can, try to use gin that incorporates lavender as a prominent botanical. You'll surely appreciate the balance of flavors achieved by balancing the gin itself with both the garnish and the liqueur.

2 oz gin

2 oz lemonade

1 splash lavender liqueur

1 splash club soda

1 lavender sprig (garnish)

1 Add the gin, lemonade, and lavender liqueur to a cocktail shaker filled with ice. Shake vigorously.

2 Strain the resulting mixture into a Mason jar filled with ice. Top with a splash of club soda and garnish with a sprig of lavender. Enjoy!

VARIATION

Instead of lemonade, you can use a flavored seltzer of your choosing to mix up the flavor. Just don't use anything too aggressive—you don't want to risk drowning out the delicate flavor of the lavender.

Basilisk

Basil and lemon are two distinctly different flavors, but together they can add an exciting new twist to a classic gin and tonic. The basil lends a refreshing herbal quality to the drink, while the tartness of the lemon helps elevate the drink above its humble origins. The Basilisk isn't a flashy drink, but it sits beautifully in the glass, providing a treat for both the eyes and the palate.

2 basil leaves

1 oz lemon juice

2 oz gin

4 oz tonic water

1 lemon twist (garnish)

Basil leaves (garnish)

1 Tear both basil leaves in half. Rub them over the rim of your Mason jar before depositing them at the bottom.

2 Add the lemon juice to the Mason jar and muddle with the basil leaves.

3 Fill the Mason jar approximately halfway with ice. Add the gin and tonic water and stir lightly.

4 Garnish with a twist of lemon and extra basil leaves if desired. Enjoy!

All Ginned Up

This take on a classic Gin Martini fills out the traditional sipper with some fruit flavor and a bit of club soda. All Ginned Up ups the ante with an extra splash of booze, but lessens the bite with a welcome bit of fizz. This cocktail is a modern take on an old classic, playing with not just flavor, but color as well; the deep purple of the liqueur and the bright green of the mint garnish create a beautiful visual within the glass.

3 oz gin

½ oz dry vermouth

½ oz blackberry liqueur

2 oz club soda

Mint leaves (garnish)

1 Fill your Mason jar approximately halfway with ice and add the gin and dry vermouth. Stir lightly.

2 Add the blackberry liqueur, but do not stir. Top with the club soda.

3 Garnish with fresh mint leaves and enjoy!

WHISKEY-BASED COCKTAILS

Most whiskey fans prefer to drink their liquor of choice straight, or at least in the form of simple cocktails like the Old Fashioned. No need for bells and whistles with whiskey—if you like the flavor, you want to savor it.

That's not to say that there aren't a whole host of fantastic whiskey cocktails out there. You might just have to look a little harder. In fact, chances are you've had one or two of them. Whiskey comes in a bit under the radar with a morning creation of its own (the famous Irish Coffee), as well as the Mint Julep, well-known for its long-standing association with the Kentucky Derby.

Whiskey drinks are a real opportunity to show off your creative side. No matter which cocktail you're making, that prominent whiskey flavor is going to be the focal point around which all other flavors revolve. You can't mask it, and if you're a whiskey lover, you don't want to. Whiskey cocktails are all about accentuating the flavors that are already there, and, as you'll see in the following pages, that can be done in a variety of different ways.

Mason Jar Mint Julep

Known far and wide as the drink of choice at the Kentucky Derby, it should come as no surprise that the bourbon-based cocktail is a Southern classic. Bourbon aficionados tend to love the Mint Julep—unsurprising, since the drink is almost pure bourbon. Don't be afraid to try one just because you're not the biggest bourbon fan in the world, though. The mint and sugar do a surprisingly good job with balancing the flavor, so it's worth a try for just about anybody! For this Mason jar version, add a splash of mint schnapps to enhance the mint taste. Sure, this might upset the purists, but so would serving a Mint Julep out of a Mason jar!

6 mint leaves

1 dash powdered sugar

1 part water

3 parts bourbon

1 splash mint schnapps

1 mint sprig (garnish)

1 Muddle the mint, sugar, and water in the bottom of your Mason jar.

2 Fill the remainder of the jar with ice.

3 Add the bourbon and mint schnapps, then garnish with a mint sprig. Enjoy!

VARIATIONS

Try adding a splash or two of different liqueurs to liven up your Mint Julep! Especially if you're looking to offset the pure bourbon flavor a bit, fruit liqueurs can go a long way toward improving the cocktail's drinkability. In particular, peach and blackberry flavors work really well with mint. Of course, you don't have to go the liqueur route. A bit of mango nectar or grapefruit juice is just as good.

Virgin Mint Julep

The Virgin Mint Julep is perfect for a sober Derby day. It's impossible to recreate the taste of bourbon with anything but bourbon, and in this case it's best not to even try. Instead, switch in a little ginger ale and lemon, and you'll still enjoy the flavorful mint accent.

6 mint leaves

1 dash powdered sugar

½ lemon (juiced)

1 oz part water

3 oz parts ginger ale

1 mint sprig (garnish)

1 Muddle the mint leaves, sugar, lemon juice, and water in the bottom of your Mason jar.

2 Fill the remainder of the jar with ice.

3 Add the ginger ale and garnish with a mint sprig. Enjoy!

Whiskey Sunset

Whiskey is far from the easiest liquor to use in a summer sipper, but with a little white wine to take the edge off, the Whiskey Sunset succeeds admirably. The Whiskey Sunset incorporates a few extra sweet-and-sour notes to create a delicious and well-rounded concoction.

2 oz bourbon

2 oz white wine

1 oz lemonade

1 splash simple syrup (page 190)

3 oz ginger ale

1 lemon wheel (garnish)

1 Fill your Mason jar with ice and all the liquid ingredients except the ginger ale. Stir thoroughly, then top with the ginger ale.

2 Garnish with a lemon wheel (feel free to add some extra lemon wheels inside the drink itself) and enjoy!

Renegade Lemonade

Nothing will make you feel like a rebel faster than drinking spiked lemonade out of a Mason jar. As if the jars themselves don't have enough of a rural feel to them, this country favorite is perfect for picnics, relaxing on the beach, or even just cooling off on the back porch. It's a simple recipe, but sometimes the simplest drinks are the most satisfying. You'll quickly find yourself going back for seconds.

1 cup simple syrup (page 190)

6 lemons (juiced)

1 cup whiskey

4 cups cold water

4 mint sprigs (garnish)

8–12 lemon wheels (garnish)

1 Add ice to a half-gallon pitcher and add the simple syrup. Add the lemon juice and whiskey, then top off with the water. Stir until thoroughly mixed.

2 Pour into four Mason jars and garnish them with sprigs of mint, plus a few lemon wheels both inside and outside the jars. Enjoy!

As with regular lemonade, there are plenty of ways to mix things up. You can adjust the sugar and lemon juice levels to increase or decrease the sweet and sour elements of the drink. Whiskey mixes surprisingly well with lemonade, and if you're an adventurous soul who feels like spiking the alcohol levels a bit more, go for it!

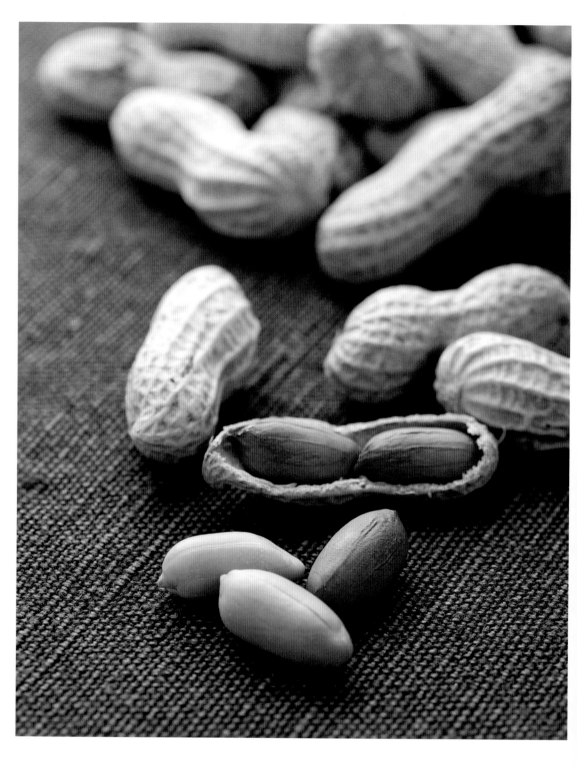

Whiskey Nut

If you're from the South, chances are you've dropped a handful of peanuts into your cola before. Why this is just a Southern tradition is a mystery; people everywhere are well aware of the delicious combo that is sugar and salt. The Whiskey Nut takes the sweet and salty partnership and adds a dose of whiskey and orange to give you something new and impressive to show off.

2 oz whiskey

1 splash orange liqueur

2 drops peanut extract

6 oz cola

1 orange wheel (garnish)

1 handful peanuts (garnish)

1 Fill your Mason jar halfway with ice and add the whiskey and orange liqueur (just enough to taste).

2 Add two drops of the peanut extract and fill with the cola.

3 Garnish with an orange wheel and a handful of peanuts. You can either eat them on the side or pop them right into the jar like you would with a can of cola. Enjoy!

Although it might seem a little odd to drop nuts directly into your drink, when you consider the popularity of almond liqueurs and flavor additives such as hazelnut, it starts to make a little more sense. Creating a drink with an appropriate balance between salty and sweet is a rewarding challenge, and nutty flavors are a great way to go about it!

Bourbon Sweet Tea

More than anything else, sweet tea might be the number-one symbol of the American South. And with bourbon's famous Kentucky roots, it was surely only a matter of time before the Bourbon Sweet Tea combination rose to prominence. It's an incredibly sweet cocktail—with the healthy dose of sugar present in the sweet tea running the risk of overwhelming the unfamiliar palate—but one that will make you feel like you just walked off a Texas cattle ranch.

1 lemon slice

2 mint leaves

1 part bourbon

4 parts sweet tea

2 or 3 lemon wheels (garnish)

1 In a small glass, muddle the lemon slice and mint leaves in the bourbon to release the flavors.

2 Add ice to your Mason jar (you'll want a lot of it) and strain the bourbon mixture into it.

3 Top with the sweet tea and pop a few lemon wheels right into the drink. Enjoy!

While store-bought sweet tea is fine, you really should try to make your own. It's usually made in large batches: throw a few of your favorite tea bags into a proportional amount of water, bring it to a boil, and let it sit for a few hours. Don't forget to add quite a bit of sugar—after all, that's what puts the sweet in sweet tea.

CROWD-PLEASER

When whipping up a large batch of Bourbon Sweet Tea, just keep the bourbon and sweet tea in 1:4 proportions. Squeeze a lemon or two into the mix if you want—you'll definitely want to put some lemon wheels in the bowl for presentation, at least. Keep the mint leaves off to the side. You don't want them getting soggy and settling to the bottom of the bowl. It won't be very appetizing, and keeping them to the side is a nice way to let people customize their own drinks.

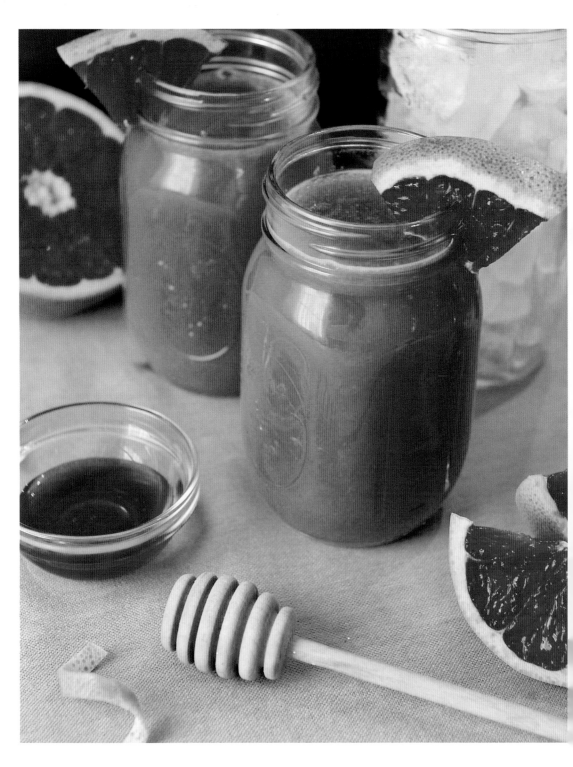

Brown Derby

Let's take things to a classy place with the Brown Derby, a classic whiskey cocktail that doesn't try too hard to overwhelm you with complex flavors. Made with grapefruit juice, whiskey, and honey, this simple and refreshing cocktail proves that when it comes to ingredients, less is often more. The Brown Derby allows the sweet grapefruit juice to play off the whiskey, dulling the sharp edge of the grapefruit flavor only slightly with the addition of a spoonful of honey.

2 oz maple whiskey

2 oz grapefruit juice

½ oz honey

1 grapefruit slice (garnish)

1 Fill a cocktail shaker with ice and add the maple whiskey, grapefruit juice, and honey. Shake vigorously until thoroughly mixed.

2 Add ice to your Mason jar and strain the cocktail shaker into it.

3 Garnish with a slice of grapefruit (leave the rind on) and enjoy!

To add another element of sweetness, take a little bit of extra honey and rim the jar with sugar.

Hot Toddy

Whiskey is the perfect liquor choice for autumn or winter, because it lends itself so well to warm drinks. While you could simply spike a mug of warm apple cider or add a dose to your hot chocolate, the Hot Toddy is a classic cocktail passed down through the ages. With a more well-rounded flavor than those simple suggestions, this classic is sure to warm you up quickly after a long day of snowshoeing. Customize this winter favorite with a little added mint flavor!

1 part honey

2 mint leaves

4 parts tea

2 parts whiskey

Lemon juice to taste

1 Add the honey to your Mason jar, allowing it time to spread across the bottom of the jar. Muddle the mint leaves into it.

2 Boil some water and make a serving of your favorite tea. Set aside.

3 Add the whiskey and lemon juice to your Mason jar. Use as much lemon as you might typically take with your tea.

4 Top the drink off with the tea you set aside earlier. Stir together lightly and enjoy!

Irish Coffee

Don't burn yourself on this one! Irish Coffee is a classic morning cocktail that will get you up and moving quick. Although the drink is little more than spiked coffee, it has taken on a life of its own in the mixology world. Brown sugar, whipped cream, nutmeg, and who knows how many other flavor variations have been thrown into the mix. But why complicate things? This classic Irish Coffee recipe will get you ready to face the day in style.

3 parts coffee

1 dash sugar

1 part Irish whiskey

1 part Irish cream

1 dollop whipped cream (garnish, optional)

1 Pour the coffee into your Mason jar and add the sugar. Stir until the sugar has dissolved completely.

2 Continue stirring and add the Irish whiskey.

3 Top with the Irish cream. Layer the cream on top, if you can. Do not stir.

4 If desired, garnish with a dollop of whipped cream on top. Enjoy!

VARIATIONS

+ The original Irish Coffee recipe from the early 1900s called for brown sugar rather than regular sugar. Go ahead and try it!

+ Use heavy cream instead of Irish cream if you want less booze.

Irish Rose

It's a bit unusual to see whiskey combined with fruity mixers, but the Irish Rose defies convention. Seemingly tailor-made for Mason jar presentation, this cocktail will dazzle any gathering with its rosy red hue. You'll almost forget you're drinking whiskey, making the Irish Rose the perfect choice to give your guests something new and exciting.

2 parts Irish whiskey

3 parts lemon-lime soda

1 lime wedge (juiced)

1 lemon wedge (juiced)

1 part grenadine

1 lime wedge (garnish)

1 Add ice to your Mason jar. Add the Irish whiskey and lemon-lime soda.

2 Squeeze the juice from one lime wedge and one lemon wedge into the drink, then top with the grenadine. Stir until thoroughly mixed.

3 Garnish with another lime wedge and enjoy!

VARIATION

Don't have grenadine? You can create a makeshift Irish Rose by substituting some cherry soda in place of the grenadine and lemon-lime soda. It won't taste the same, but it will still be delicious!

Even though it contains no alcohol, grenadine is a must-have addition to any home bar. Typically made from red currants and pomegranate, grenadine is often added for presentation as much as taste, thanks to its uncommonly bright coloration.

Thornless Rose

The Irish Rose is a delicious drink, but some might say the whiskey seems out of place. So why not mix yourself up a delicious virgin version of the same drink? Just as flavorful and featuring even brighter colors, the Thornless Rose is a fizzy and fruity drink that anyone can enjoy.

½ lemon (juiced)

½ lime (juiced)

1 part grenadine

3 parts club soda

1 lime wedge (garnish)

1 Add ice to your Mason jar, then squeeze in the lemon and lime juice.

2 Add the grenadine and club soda, then stir until thoroughly mixed.

3 Garnish with a lime wedge and enjoy!

VARIATIONS

Grenadine is typically made with pomegranate juice, but you can feel free to substitute cherry juice (or cherry soda), if you prefer something a little more familiar.

Mason Jar Bourbon Press

A classic cocktail for whiskey lovers, the Bourbon Press is a perfect drink for anytime and anywhere. It's even at home outdoors, right down to its appearance: it looks like nothing so much as a glass of lemonade or iced tea. The Bourbon Press is the perfect drink to take to the park while you relax with a good book. Screw a lid on that Mason jar and head out there!

2 oz bourbon

1 dash orange bitters

2 oz ginger ale

2 oz club soda

1 lemon slice (garnish)

1 Add a few good-sized ice cubes to your Mason jar and pour in the bourbon.

2 Add a quick dash of orange bitters.

3 Fill the remainder of the jar with the ginger ale and club soda. Garnish with a slice of lemon and enjoy!

VARIATIONS

If bourbon isn't your thing, you can also feel free to substitute Scotch or rye whiskey, depending on your preference.

Mason Jar Whiskey Sour

Traditionally, a Whiskey Sour is made with whiskey, lemon juice, and simple syrup, but orange juice is a popular addition to make the drink feel like more of a "punch." This is the approach taken by the Mason jar version, giving the Mason Jar Whiskey Sour a bit more body than its traditional counterpart and making it an unexpectedly perfect brunch option. Whiskey for brunchy—why not?

2 cups orange juice

1 cup whiskey

½ cup orange liqueur

½ cup lemon juice

¼ cup simple syrup
(page 190)

Orange slices (garnish)

1 Add ice to a pitcher and pour the liquid ingredients in. Stir until thoroughly combined.

2 Add ice to each Mason jar and pour the desired amount. Garnish with orange slices and enjoy!

The Highland Coconut

Scotch and coconut water has become a popular combination in the Caribbean. Ideally, this cocktail is made with fresh coconut water, but since that can be difficult to come by in other parts of the world, its bottled alternative will work just fine. While purists would argue that Scotch and coconut water are all you need, the Mason jar version opts for a splash of lime juice to add the smallest jolt of citrus.

2 oz Scotch whiskey

2 oz coconut water

1 splash lime juice

1 lime twist (garnish)

1 Add ice to your Mason jar and combine the Scotch whiskey and coconut water. Stir lightly.

2 Top with a splash of lime juice, and garnish with a twist of lime if desired. Enjoy!

MAKES 1 SERVING.

Old Reliable

"Whiskey and Coke" is a classic combination, but most will agree that it lacks a certain element of flair. Still, sometimes you want a cocktail that is simple, straightforward, and reliable. Something you can count on. Old Reliable takes whiskey and cola and adds just a little something more, taking this favorite from college bars across the country and elevating it into a classier drinking experience for the modern age.

2 oz whiskey

6 oz cola

1 oz orange liqueur

1 splash lime juice

Orange wheel (garnish)

1 Add ice to your Mason jar and combine the whiskey, cola, and orange liqueur. Stir thoroughly.

2 Top with a splash of lime juice and garnish with an orange wheel. Enjoy!

Respect Your Elders

Elderflower liqueur isn't a staple, but you've almost certainly seen the distinctively shaped bottles of St. Germain populating the shelves of your local liquor store. It's a sweet liqueur best used in moderation, but it goes extremely well with both whiskey and lemon juice. The Respect Your Elders will give you a newfound appreciation for what elderflower brings to the table. After trying this one, you might just have to keep a bottle around.

3 oz whiskey

1 oz elderflower liqueur

1 oz sweet vermouth

½ oz lemon juice

½ oz splash simple syrup (page 190)

1 splash club soda

Lemon twist (garnish)

1 Add the whiskey, elderflower liqueur, sweet vermouth, lemon juice, and simple syrup to a cocktail shaker filled with ice. Shake vigorously.

2 Strain the resulting mixture into a Mason jar field with ice. Top with a splash of club soda.

3 Garnish with a lemon twist and enjoy!

VARIATION

Instead of club soda, a splash of ginger ale can give this cocktail a little something extra. The ginger pairs very well with the elderflower, but it does change the flavor profile of the cocktail quite a bit.

MAKES 1 SERVING.

Scotch Highball

Technically, "Highball" could refer to any cocktail in the "and soda" family: vodka and soda, Scotch and soda, whiskey and soda, etc. But there's something about the Scotch Highball that makes it stand apart. Maybe it's the distinctive, peaty flavor of the Scotch. Maybe it's the golden color. Whatever the reason, the Scotch Highball is beautiful in its simplicity. Is a Highball still a Highball if it isn't served in a Highball glass? For the sake of the Scotch Highball, let's say yes.

2 oz Scotch whiskey

4 oz club soda

Lemon twist (garnish)

1 Fill your Mason jar with ice and add the Scotch whiskey. Add the club soda.

2 Garnish with a twist of lemon and enjoy!

VARIATIONS

As the recipe indicates, a Scotch Highball is just another name for Scotch and soda. There are plenty of other cocktails that fit the same mold, so whether your preference is vodka, whiskey, rum, or tequila, there's a Highball to suit your palate.

Cherry Highball

As stated within the Scotch Highball recipe, a Highball can be any liquor and club soda. But really, why should it have to be liquor at all? People have been making Italian sodas with club soda and flavored syrup for generations, and with good reason—they are delicious. The Cherry Highball chooses cherry syrup, but there's really no reason you couldn't make a Virgin Highball of your choice with any syrup you have on hand.

1 oz cherry syrup

6 oz club soda

1 maraschino cherry (garnish)

1 Fill your Mason jar with ice and add the cherry syrup and club soda. Stir thoroughly.

2 Garnish with a maraschino cherry and enjoy!

VARIATION

Although this recipe calls for cherry, other fruited syrups will work equally well. Blueberry, blackberry, and peach are particularly good, but you can get even more creative with maple syrup, honey, and other flavors if you are so inclined.

Salted Caramel Apple

Caramel apples are a longtime staple of state fairs, fall festivals, and, of course, Halloween celebrations. But why risk breaking your teeth on an uncooperative caramel apple when you can enjoy the same great flavor in cocktail form? The Salted Caramel Apple is best in small doses. Although it won't fill your Mason jar to the brim, it packs a seriously flavorful punch into a few delicious sips. It's a cocktail that conjures fond memories of crisp autumn days.

Salt (for rimming)

2 oz whiskey

1 oz sweet apple liqueur

1 oz caramel liqueur

1 apple slice (garnish)

1 Use the salt to rim the edge of your Mason jar.

2 Add the whiskey, apple liqueur, and caramel liqueur to a cocktail shaker filled with ice. Shake vigorously.

3 Fill your Mason jar with ice and strain the whiskey mixture into it.

4 Garnish with a slice of apple and enjoy!

BEER-BASED COCKTAILS

Not all cocktails have to be liquor based. You might be familiar with beer cocktails, such as the Summer Shandy, which introduces a sweet element in the form of lemonade. Beer might not sound like it lends itself particularly well to cocktails, but it actually makes a fair amount of sense. Citrus beers are among the industry's best sellers, and flavors like chocolate and honey are frequently introduced to the brewing process.

In fact, beer cocktails are some of the easiest to make. Rarely containing more than two or three ingredients, they're the perfect way to add maximum flair with minimum effort. If you don't just feel like cracking open a beer after work, a nice beer cocktail might make you feel a bit more accomplished.

Depending on the season, there are a variety of different options to choose from, each more delicious than the last.

Summer Shandy

Far and away the most popular of the beer-based cocktails, the Shandy is a crisp and refreshing drink to enjoy during the hottest months of the year. The summery freshness of lemonade will provide the perfect augment to your favorite seasonal beer, leaving you with the ideal beverage to sip while relaxing on the patio.

2 parts beer (wheat beer, lager, or pilsner)

1 part lemonade

1 lemon wedge (garnish)

1 Pour your chosen beer into your Mason jar. Wheat beers, lagers, and pilsners are the most common choices, as darker beers will not interact well with the lemonade.

2 Top with the lemonade.

3 Add ice if desired and garnish with a lemon wedge. Enjoy!

VARIATIONS

+ **Shandygaff:** To make this popular British variation of the Shandy, swap out the lemonade in favor of carbonated ginger ale or ginger beer.

+ **Lager Top:** Another British variation, this one is made specifically with a lager beer and topped with just a splash of lemonade.

The Summer Shandy is the perfect outdoor cocktail for a picnic. Try dressing up your Mason jar with different summery accents, such as a checkered ribbon to mimic a picnic blanket. If you're feeling industrious, slice up some fresh, brightly colored fruits and layer them in an empty jar to create a gorgeous rainbow centerpiece.

Lemon Cooler

The Summer Shandy is a great summer treat, but it can get a little old after a while. After all, it's just beer and lemonade—how creative can you really get? Well, the answer is: at least a little. For a stronger, sweeter option, reopen the liquor cabinet and make yourself a Lemon Cooler.

8 oz Summer Shandy (page 245)

1 oz whiskey

1 spoonful honey

1 splash lemon juice

1 lemon slice (garnish)

1 Add ice to your Mason jar and make yourself a Summer Shandy (page 245).

2 Add the whiskey, honey, and lemon juice and stir until all ingredients are thoroughly mixed.

3 Garnish with a slice of lemon and enjoy!

VARIATIONS

+ Some whiskey brands make their own honey whiskey variant. Feel free to use this in place of the honey and whiskey, but know that the taste won't be as pure as if you use real honey.

+ On a similar note, some breweries bottle their own Shandy beers. If there's one you particularly like, try using that as the base for this cocktail.

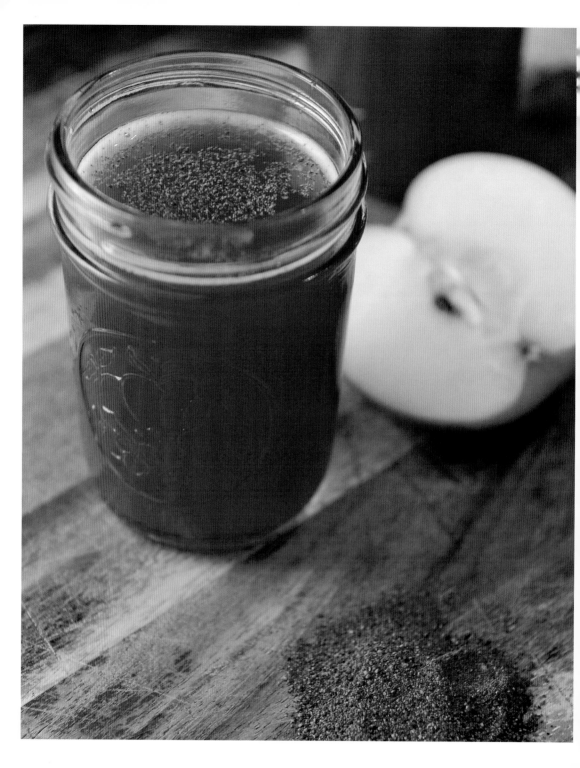

MAKES 1 SERVING.

Fall Shandy

Lemonade may be out of season by the time the leaves start dropping from the trees, but nothing says fall like a slice of pumpkin pie and a glass of fresh apple cider. Well, why not combine both of those flavors? Using the pumpkin beer of your choice and the best fresh apple cider you can find, try something a little different this fall.

2 parts pumpkin beer

1 part fresh apple cider

Dusting of nutmeg

1 In a simple 2:1 ratio, add your favorite pumpkin beer to your Mason jar, along with the fresh apple cider.

2 Hit the top with a dusting of nutmeg and enjoy!

VARIATIONS

+ Some variations call for sparkling cider rather than the regular stuff, but it adds a bit of a sharpness that threatens to overwhelm the pumpkin flavor of the beer.

+ If you want to take things up a notch with a real boozy treat, you can always use hard cider. Beware, though: this will make your drink considerably stronger than it tastes.

Winter Shandy

You've tried the Summer Shandy and the Fall Shandy, but have you ever heard of a Winter Shandy? Where the Summer Shandy uses lemonade and the Fall Shandy opts for apple cider, the Winter Shandy eschews fruit entirely and dives straight into a warm, cozy pool of hot chocolate. This time, you'll want to grab a bottle of your favorite stout to add a boozy edge to this winter favorite. Adding liquor to hot chocolate is a time-honored tradition, but using beer lessens the bite and provides a more well-rounded flavor profile for this delicious cocktail. You may want to use a Mason jar with a handle, and be careful not to burn yourself when drinking this delightfully warm treat.

6 oz hot chocolate

3 oz stout beer

Whipped cream (garnish)

Marshmallows (garnish)

1 Pour the hot chocolate and stout beer into your Mason jar. Lightly stir.

2 Top with the whipped cream and marshmallows if desired and enjoy!

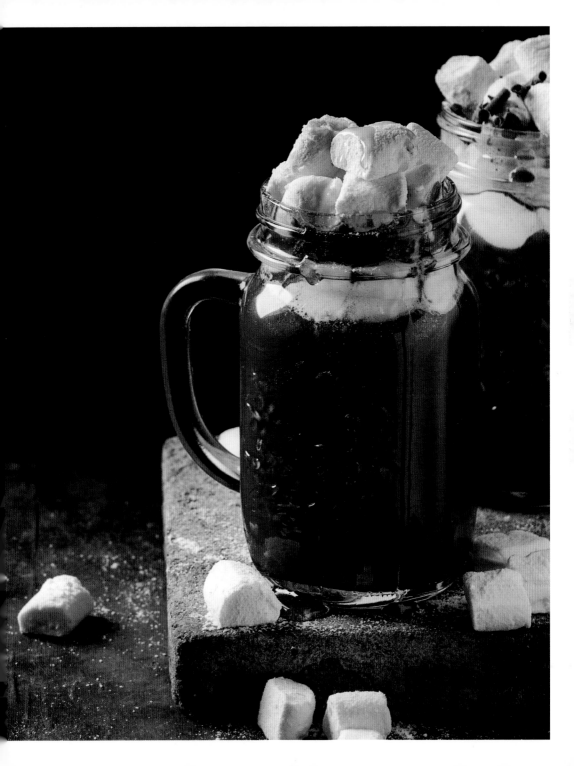

Ginger Shandy

Why limit your Shandy options to the standard? Most people don't think of beer as an alcohol that needs to be mixed or otherwise altered, but there are countless interesting and inventive ways to spice up your beer consumption. Lemonade is the standard Summer Shandy addition, but maybe you want a little more carbonation. Ginger beer is the perfect complement to lighter beers, adding a bit of spice and a nice fizzy kick to your beverage.

1 small handful mint leaves

2 parts wheat beer

1 part ginger beer

1 lemon slice (garnish)

1 Add ice to your Mason jar. Rub the mint leaves along the rim, then tear them in half and add them to the jar.

2 Pour in your wheat beer.

3 Top with the ginger beer and garnish with a slice of lemon. Enjoy!

VARIATIONS

+ You can add more or less ginger beer, according to your preference. The strong taste of ginger beer means it's probably better to err on the side of caution.

+ If ginger beer isn't your thing, you can always opt for ginger ale instead; however, the less assertive taste of ginger ale won't be as apparent, and you run the risk of feeling like you've just watered down your beer.

Black Velvet

It's not every day that it makes sense to drink champagne out of a Mason jar, but the Black Velvet will give you just such an occasion. This is not a subtle cocktail: the dark beer layered with the light champagne creates a dividing line of flavor that couldn't possibly be more clear. Eventually, the two ingredients will blend together, creating a beautiful mahogany-colored drink that tastes as good as it looks.

1 part champagne

1 splash sparkling cider

1 part stout beer

1 Pour the champagne into your Mason jar.

2 Add in a splash of sparkling cider.

3 Using the back of a spoon, layer the stout beer on top of the champagne. Try not to allow the two ingredients to mix. Enjoy!

Some versions call for the champagne to be floated atop the stout, rather than vice versa. As you drink, the ingredients will mix together regardless of which way you chose to assemble them, so this is down to personal preference.

Mason Jar Michelada

A cousin of the Bloody Mary, the Michelada is a popular brunch cocktail that features beer rather than liquor. Traditionally made with a Mexican beer, the Michelada otherwise includes a similar blend of tomato juice, lime, hot sauce, and other flavors to create a unique drinking experience. Like the Bloody Mary, the Michelada is highly customizable and should be crafted according to the preferences of the drinker—but the Mason Jar Michelada will get you started just fine.

1 lime wedge (for rimming)

Salt (for rimming)

4 oz tomato juice

1 splash lime juice

1 splash Worcestershire sauce

1 splash hot sauce

4 oz Mexican beer

1 lime wedge (garnish)

1 Rub the cut side of a lime wedge along the edge of your Mason jar before rimming with the salt.

2 Fill your Mason jar approximately halfway with ice, then add the tomato juice, lime juice, Worcestershire sauce, and hot sauce. Stir thoroughly.

3 Top with the Mexican beer. Garnish with a lime wedge and enjoy!

Traditionally, a Michelada is served with the remaining beer still in the bottle. As you drink, periodically top off your Michelada with the remaining beer until it is gone. This creates a unique drinking experience, since the flavor of the cocktail will continue to evolve over time as the ratio of ingredients changes.

MISCELLANEOUS COCKTAILS

Sometimes you need something a little bit stronger to get you through the day. Once in a while, a regular old vodka or whiskey drink can't get the job done. If you need a little extra kick in the pants, try one of these combination cocktails, featuring delicious blends of multiple alcohol types.

Of course, not all of them are outrageously strong. Some are quite the opposite. The Long Island Iced Tea might be the perfect cocktail to enhance your own buzz, but a little Mason Jar Sangria is the perfect social cocktail to augment any gathering of friends.

The beauty of so many of these is that there's nearly infinite room for customization. Sangria in particular lends itself to the whims of the drinker, as just about any combination of fruits can be included, but anything containing a high volume of several different liquors can be tweaked and twisted this way and that. Show off your creativity! Serving your drinks in Mason jars already reveals a bit of your personality. Isn't it time for your drinks to reflect that too?

Grand Slam

The Grand Slam, so named for the four different liquors incorporated into the boozy body of the drink, is a bottle with a message in it. That message is "beware." Something of a sister cocktail to the Long Island Iced Tea, the Grand Slam is a drink delicious enough to make you forget how strong it is. It's a cocktail designed to give you a nice buzz, but be careful serving it to friends who might not be aware of its alcohol content. With just cola and lime as mixers, the Grand Slam is a pragmatist's dream: simple, uncomplicated, and delicious.

½ oz vodka

½ oz rum

½ oz tequila

½ oz orange liqueur

1 lime wedge (juiced)

4 oz cola

1 lime wedge (garnish)

1 Add ice to your Mason jar and pour in the vodka, rum, tequila, and orange liqueur.

2 Squeeze in the juice from one lime wedge, then top the drink off with the cola.

3 Garnish with a lime wedge and enjoy!

Mason Jar Sidecar

Although the original recipe is considerably more complex, the Mason Jar Sidecar has been refined into a simple, three-ingredient drink. Made famous by the legendary Harry's New York Bar in Paris, the brandy-based cocktail is widely regarded as one of the best to come out of the Prohibition years.

Sugar (for rimming)

1 lemon wedge (for rimming)

1 part orange liqueur

1 part lemon juice

2 parts brandy

1 orange slice (garnish)

1 Rim the edge of your Mason jar by rubbing it with the lemon wedge and dipping it in the sugar.

2 Pour the liquid ingredients into a cocktail shaker filled with ice and shake well.

3 Strain into your Mason jar and garnish with an orange slice. Enjoy!

There is considerable disagreement regarding the proper proportions of the drink's ingredients, with many firmly believing that the ingredients should be used in equal measure. This largely comes down to personal taste or how strong you would like your drink to be.

Americano

Originally called the Milano-Torino (after the Italian cities in which it first gained popularity), the Americano took its new name during the Prohibition years, when the drink became a favorite of American tourists. The Americano is actually the first drink ever ordered by James Bond in Ian Fleming's celebrated novels, despite his later penchant for vodka martinis. Although the Americano doesn't normally include an orange component, spice up the Mason jar version with a little added sweetness to this typically bitter drink.

1 oz Campari

1 oz sweet vermouth

1 oz orange liqueur

6 oz club soda

1 lemon or orange twist (garnish)

1 Fill your Mason jar with ice and pour in the Campari, sweet vermouth, and orange liqueur.

2 Layer in the club soda until the jar is nearly filled.

3 Garnish with your choice of fruit twist and enjoy!

VARIATIONS

Negroni: The Americano is considered an offshoot of the Negroni, which is a considerably stronger cocktail, made by discarding the club soda in favor of gin.

Cocktail recipes often call for citrus twists, which can be a challenge to perfect. The most basic method simply involves using a vegetable peeler to slice off a strip of zest. However, if you're looking to class up your drink with an impressive, curling twist, it's going to take a bit more effort. Using a V-shaped blade, slice into your chosen fruit and drag the blade in a spiral pattern around the outside. If done correctly, you should be left with a long, curled strip of zest.

Long Island Iced Tea

Ah, the legendary Long Island Iced Tea. Legendary among even the strongest of mixed drinks. Despite the fact that there are countless Long Island Iced Tea recipes floating around, they all have one thing in common: an astonishing amount of booze. The Long Island Iced Tea is the perfect cocktail to have one of and quit while you're ahead...but they're so delicious, you might not be able to say no to a second.

1 part vodka

1 part light rum

1 part gin

1 part silver tequila

1 part triple sec

1 part lemon juice

1 tsp sugar

2 parts cola

1 lemon slice (garnish)

1 Add all the ingredients (except for the cola and lemon slice) into a cocktail shaker filled with ice. Shake until frothy.

2 Fill your Mason jar with your desired amount of ice and strain the mixture into it. Top with the cola and garnish with a slice of lemon. Enjoy!

VARIATIONS

Most variations center around the lemon juice and cola. Some opt to use only orange juice, while others use (as the name of the cocktail might suggest) real iced tea. Some simply use less cola (just a splash!), while others use sweet-and-sour mix. It's up to you to decide which of these sounds best to you, but the recipe above might be the tastiest.

Non Island Iced Tea

A nonalcoholic Long Island Iced Tea seems almost like an oxymoron, but the joy of the Long Island Iced Tea centers largely around the fact that it just doesn't taste like alcohol. With that in mind, it shouldn't be too difficult to recreate the flavor profile sans booze—and many have!

1 part iced tea (unsweetened)

1 part lemonade

1 part cola

1 lemon wedge (garnish)

1 Add as much ice as you want and combine the liquid ingredients in your Mason jar. Stir until completely mixed.

2 Garnish with a lemon wedge and enjoy!

VARIATIONS

There are many variants on nonalcoholic Long Island Ice Tea, but this one most closely matches the Long Island Iced Tea recipe in this book. Others incorporate apple cider, ginger ale, pure lemon juice, and a plethora of other ingredients. What you choose to adhere to will probably depend on which Long Island Iced Tea recipe you prefer.

CROWD-PLEASER

As far as nonalcoholic drinks go, you could definitely do worse than offering the Non Island Iced Tea as a party punch. Just keep the iced tea, lemonade, and cola in approximately equal parts, and you'll have an unusual drink that will serve as both a refreshing beverage and a unique conversation starter.

Iced Coffee Explosion

Irish Coffee is delicious, but what if you're in the mood for iced coffee? This alternative is layered with several different types of alcohol, creating a medley of flavors that stand up well to even the strongest coffee. This is a cocktail strong enough to knock you down, but with more than enough caffeine kick to get you right back up again.

1 oz whiskey

1 oz Irish cream liqueur

1 oz dark rum

6 oz iced coffee

Cream and sugar as needed

1 Fill your Mason jar approximately halfway with ice and add the whiskey, Irish cream liqueur, dark rum, and iced coffee. Stir until mixed.

2 Depending on how you prefer your coffee, add cream and/or sugar as needed and enjoy!

Cherry Hooker

A variation of the Screwdriver, it's not entirely clear how the Cherry Hooker took its slightly uncouth name. Regardless, it's no surprise that the cherry and orange flavors play off each other very well. There's a reason that orange juice is such a common cocktail mixer, and, as with the Mimosa or Screwdriver, the Cherry Hooker is a common morning cocktail. Whether it's to shake off last night's hangover or to start your Saturday with a bang, it's hard to say no to this delicious classic. In fact, why not personalize it with a little squirt of lime juice? Lime is the traditional garnish for the Cherry Hooker anyway, so go ahead and add a bit to the drink itself.

3 oz cherry brandy

Orange juice to fill

1 splash lime juice

1 lime wheel (garnish)

1 Pour the liquid ingredients into a cocktail shaker filled with ice and shake well.

2 Add some ice to your Mason jar and strain the resulting mixture over it.

3 Garnish with a lime wheel and enjoy!

VARIATIONS

+ **Cherry Sunrise:** One popular variation involves adding a splash of grenadine at the very end. This is a purely aesthetic choice, and if you're a fan of the Tequila Sunrise look, you should give it a try.

+ Other garnishes range from lemon wedges to maraschino cherries to orange twists. As with most garnishes, only you can decide which sounds best to you.

Mason Jar Sangria

Like the Bloody Mary, Sangria is a cocktail with about a million different variations. Everyone loves to put their own spin on it, and that's part of what makes it so great. When it comes to Mason jar cocktails, sometimes you want more than just a classic cocktail repackaged. Sangria is the perfect homespun and customizable drink to encapsulate the rustic, self-sufficient attitude that the Mason jar conveys.

1 bottle red wine

6 oz brandy

4 oz simple syrup (page 190)

4 oz orange juice

1 apple (peeled, cored, and diced)

1 orange (peeled and thinly sliced)

1 cup blackberries

1 lemon (cut into wheels)

1 lime (cut into wheels)

1 Combine all the ingredients (including the fruit) into a large container and seal tightly.

2 Refrigerate for about 24 hours to allow the flavors to combine.

3 Pour the resulting fruit mixture into a punch bowl, hand out Mason jars to all your friends, and enjoy!

VARIATIONS

Any and all fruit is acceptable in Sangria. The drink is essentially a fruit salad mixed with wine. Like pomegranate? Like honeydew? Throw them in! It's up to you to create the drink that best suits your tastes.

CROWD-PLEASER

Mason Jar Sangria is designed to be made in large batches. The recipe above is already intended for a half-dozen people or so, but you can double everything in the recipe to put together something for an even larger brunch party. The real joy of Sangria is the fruit, so adding more of that will never go awry!

Rainbow Sangria

At its best, Sangria is essentially fruit salad and wine. So why not take it a step further with this delicious and visually arresting white wine concoction? Rainbow Sangria takes full advantage of the Mason jar's presentation opportunities, creating such a gorgeous layered look that you (and your friends) won't be able to look away. Best of all, rather than having a few pieces of fruit to pick out of the bottom of your Sangria glass, now you have a feast!

¼ cup kiwis (sliced)

¼ cup mango (sliced)

¼ cup orange (sliced)

¼ cup strawberries (sliced)

¼ cup grapes

¼ cup blueberries

White wine to fill

1 Slice the kiwis, mango, orange, and strawberries. No need to cut them too small, but remember that you'll be layering them.

2 Add them to your Mason jar in the following order: grapes, blueberries, kiwis, mango, orange, and strawberries.

3 Pour the white wine into the gaps until your Mason jar is filled, and enjoy!

Virgin Sangria

Sangria is colorful, fruity, and delicious. So why should you have to miss out on all the fun just because you don't want to drink? This Virgin Sangria recipe packs the same flavorful punch as its alcoholic counterpart, but shifts the emphasis onto the fruit. Like fruit salad? Like fruit juice? Then give this great Sangria alternative a try.

10 oz grape juice

6 oz apple juice

4 oz orange juice

2 oz lemon juice

2 oz lime juice

1 apple (peeled, cored, and diced)

1 orange (peeled and thinly sliced)

1 cup blackberries

4 oz club soda

1 lemon (garnish, cut into wheels)

1 lime (garnish, cut into wheels)

1 Combine all the ingredients (except the club soda and lemon and lime wheels) into a large container and seal tightly. Refrigerate for about 24 hours to allow the flavors to combine.

2 Pour the resulting fruit mixture into a punch bowl.

3 Before drinking, add four ounces of club soda to your drink for just a hint of carbonation. Stir it up, garnish your Mason jar with a lemon wheel or lime wheel, and enjoy!

As with regular Sangria, feel free to mix in any fruits you like. Whatever you think is going to be delicious after soaking in fruit juice, toss it into the fray.

Snowball

Finally, a winter drink! Advocaat is essentially the European answer to eggnog and is marketed just as well. In fact, the Snowball is such a popular "winter warmer" in Britain that many beverage companies have begun making their own prebottled Snowball drinks to sell during the winter months. While it hasn't reached this level of popularity in the United States, it's a drink worth checking out, if only to see what all the fuss is about over there. To give it an American twist, we're adding a dash of maple syrup.

1 part Advocaat

1 splash lime juice

1 dash maple syrup

1 part lemonade

1 dollop whipped cream (garnish)

1 maraschino cherry (garnish)

1 Pour the Advocaat into a cocktail shaker and add in a squeeze of lime juice. Shake thoroughly until they are mixed.

2 Add the Advocaat-and-lime mixture to your Mason jar and pour in a dash of maple syrup, then top off with the lemonade. The result should be just thick enough to support a small dollop of whipped cream as a garnish, topped with a maraschino cherry. Enjoy!

VARIATIONS

Alternate garnishes vary from dusting with nutmeg to simple lime wedges. Feel free to experiment and discover which flavors you feel best complement this unique drink.

Advocaat is fairly simple to make, with just egg, simple syrup (page 190), and brandy as its ingredients. If you're feeling adventurous (or just can't find a mass-produced option), you can always try making your own!

Alabama Slammer

Rumored to take its name from none other than famous Alabama quarterback Brett Favre, the Alabama Slammer has been a popular drink in the American South for decades. Whether its origin story is true or not, it has entered into popular culture as fact. And who's to argue? Despite carrying almost two full shots of liquor, the Alabama Slammer is a delicious medley of flavors perfect for any summer day. The drink doesn't usually call for grenadine, but why miss out on an opportunity to give it that beautiful sunset look? This cocktail is a classic, but make it your own!

¾ oz peach liqueur

¾ oz Amaretto

¾ oz sloe gin

¾ oz vodka

6 oz orange juice

1 splash grenadine

1 orange slice (garnish)

1 maraschino cherry (garnish)

1 Add your desired amount of ice to your Mason jar, then add the liquor ingredients.

2 Top off with the orange juice and a splash of grenadine, then stir until everything is thoroughly mixed.

3 Garnish with a slice of orange and a maraschino cherry and enjoy!

VARIATION

Red Death: This popular spin-off is a standard Alabama Slammer with a Kamikaze shot added to it. Be careful.

Not every variant of the Alabama Slammer includes vodka, and it isn't hard to understand why. Peach liqueur, Amaretto, and sloe gin all have very distinct flavors, while the vodka seems designed purely to boost the alcohol content. If you want something just as flavorful but not as strong, feel free to omit the vodka.

Pimm's Mason Jar

Pimm's is a popular brand of fruit cup liqueurs, and the unique nature of these beverages inspired the Pimm's Cup. There are several different iterations of the Pimm's Cup, the most well-known of which is the gin-based Pimm's Cup No. 1. Aptly named after the Pimm's No. 1 Cup liqueur, which tastes of spiced and fruit-infused gin, this Pimm's Mason Jar recipe achieves a surprising depth of flavor for a cocktail containing so few ingredients. The Pimm's Cup is also the traditional drink of Wimbledon, so if you're throwing a tennis watch party or even just feeling a little classy, this is the drink for you. If you're just making one for yourself at home, try this twist: the Pimm's Mason Jar includes a bit of cherry liqueur, for some added depth to the already strong fruit flavors.

2 oz Pimm's No. 1 Cup

4 oz lemon-lime soda

1 oz cherry liqueur

2 cucumber wheels (garnish)

1 lemon wheel (garnish)

1 Add ice to your Mason jar and pour in the Pimm's No. 1 Cup and lemon-lime soda, then add a splash of cherry liqueur. Stir until thoroughly mixed.

2 Add a couple of cucumber wheels directly into the drink. Garnish with a lemon wheel and enjoy!

MAKES 1 SERVING.

Pimm's Virgin

How can you make a virgin version of a cocktail named after a specific fruit liqueur? You try your best to recreate the medley of flavors, that's how. The Pimm's recipe is tightly guarded (only about half a dozen people in the entire world know it), so you'll probably never be able to get the flavors exactly right...but as long as you can come close, it's a drink everybody will love.

4 oz lemon-lime soda

2 oz ginger ale

1 oz cola

1 oz orange juice

½ lemon (juiced)

1 drop bitters

2 cucumber wheels (garnish)

1 lemon wheel (garnish)

1 Add ice to your Mason jar and add the liquid ingredients together, topping off with one drop of bitters. Stir until thoroughly mixed.

2 Slice two cucumber wheels and add them to the drink itself. Garnish with a lemon wheel and enjoy!

VARIATION

To recreate the gin-like qualities of the original Pimm's Cup, add a few mint leaves to the recipe.

If you like the idea of cucumber in a mocktail, try the Frozen Cucumber Melon Slush (page 297).

Blackberry Fizz

Everyone loves champagne and prosecco, but they simply aren't included in enough cocktails. But with the addition of a little liqueur, champagne can be used not only to create a delicious cocktail, but a beautiful-looking, highbrow cocktail at that! The Blackberry Fizz is a great example of two simple ingredients creating something fantastic.

6 oz champagne or prosecco

1 oz blackberry liqueur

1 mint leaf (garnish)

1 Pour the champagne into your Mason jar, filling it approximately halfway.

2 Add the blackberry liqueur (1 oz is recommended, but add to your desired level of sweetness).

3 Add ice and top with a mint leaf for garnish. Enjoy!

VARIATION

The Blackberry Fizz is a favorite, but this drink can be made with any liqueur you have handy. A Raspberry Fizz or Lemon-Lime Fizz would also be delicious, if you have the appropriate ingredients.

Champagne Float

Here's something you don't see every day: ice cream in a cocktail. Root beer floats have always been popular, and some enterprising bars and breweries have begun offering beer floats. But champagne and ice cream are a much more natural combination, with the richness of ice cream playing beautifully against the bubbly sweetness of champagne. With the addition of a little fresh fruit, the Champagne Float becomes a truly indulgent treat.

4 fresh raspberries

1 oz raspberry liqueur

1 or 2 scoops vanilla ice cream

4 oz champagne

1 Place two of the raspberries in the bottom of your Mason jar and add the raspberry liqueur. Lightly muddle them together.

2 Top with one or two scoops of vanilla ice cream, according to your preference.

3 Gently pour the champagne over the ice cream, being careful not to let it overflow.

4 Top with the remaining raspberries and enjoy!

VARIATION

Vanilla ice cream is standard in any "float," but it's not your only option. For example, you could match the ice cream to the liqueur, replacing the raspberry liqueur with strawberry liqueur and using strawberry ice cream instead of vanilla. Champagne plays well with just about any fruit, so feel free to experiment!

MAKES 1 SERVING.

Mezcal Paloma

Traditionally made with tequila, the Paloma is a cocktail full of citrus goodness, balancing the fizz of grapefruit soda with the tartness of lime. Using mezcal in place of tequila adds another flavor profile into the mix: smoke. Though similar to tequila, mezcal is known primarily for its smoky quality, which can help take the Paloma to new heights. Though it won't be for everyone, the Mezcal Paloma layers in sweetness, tartness, and smokiness for a drinking experience that is at once confounding and delightful.

2 oz mezcal

4 oz grapefruit soda

1 splash lime juice

1 lime wedge (garnish)

1 Fill your Mason jar approximately halfway with ice and add the mezcal, grapefruit soda, and lime juice. Stir until mixed.

2 Garnish with a lime wedge and enjoy!

VARIATION

Want more emphasis on the grapefruit flavor? Try replacing the grapefruit soda with grapefruit juice. The smoky flavor of the mezcal will have a much different impact against the body of the juice. Give it a try!

MORE
MOCKTAILS

There are plenty of reasons to know your nonalcoholic (or "virgin") drinks. Maybe you have kids, and you don't want them to feel left out. Maybe you have a friend who doesn't drink. Maybe you don't drink. Or maybe you just want to try something a little bit different, without adding a bunch of alcohol to the mix. Whatever your reason for trying them might be, virgin cocktails can be every bit as delicious as their boozy counterparts.

In some ways, these nonalcoholic drinks are significantly easier to work with than regular cocktails. For starters, you don't have to worry about complementing the flavor of the alcohol in question—there isn't any! Your Mason jar is a sandbox in which to experiment, combining flavor after flavor until you hit on something that works. You'll find that some of these virgin cocktails are finished products, while others are great starting points. Watermelon and lime not your thing? Try mixing in some blueberry and lemon instead!

Perhaps most important, nonalcoholic drinks are inclusive. If you're mixing drinks at a party, it's always considerate to have a nonalcoholic variant to offer to anyone who doesn't wish to partake. Whether they are hungover, a teetotaler, or a designated driver, it's always best to respect the decision of those not drinking, and being able to offer them a virgin drink is a great way to show that you care.

In this book, we've mixed most of our mocktails in alongside their boozy counterparts as virgin versions—or adaptations—so you can easily make both at once, using many of the same ingredients. You can find a quick reference to those on the next page.

QUICK REFERENCE TO VIRGIN VERSIONS

Roy Rogers

One of the most popular virgin cocktails in the world, the Roy Rogers is extremely simple to make. A simple mix of grenadine and cola, it's really not much more than a cherry cola with a pomegranate twist.

12 oz cola

1 splash grenadine

1 splash lime juice

1 maraschino cherry (garnish)

1 Add ice to your Mason jar and pour in the cola.

2 Top with a splash of grenadine and add a squeeze of lime juice.

3 Garnish with a maraschino cherry and enjoy!

Shirley Temple

Similar to the Roy Rogers, the Shirley Temple is a simple mix of grenadine and ginger ale. Ironically, the child star despised the drink that she inspired, calling it "icky." Despite this famous rebuke, the drink remains one of the most frequently ordered virgin cocktails in the world. Like the Roy Rogers, the Shirley Temple can be easily personalized with the addition of a little lemon or lime.

12 oz ginger ale

1 splash grenadine

1 splash lime juice

1 maraschino cherry (garnish)

1 Add ice to your Mason jar and pour in the ginger ale.

2 Top with a splash of grenadine and a squeeze of lime juice.

3 Garnish with a maraschino cherry and enjoy!

VARIATION

Although ginger ale is widely agreed upon as the standard base for the drink, some versions call for lemonade instead.

MAKES 1 SERVING.

Frozen Cucumber Melon Slush

What's better than a refreshing slushy when it comes to keeping cool in the summer? Sure, you could hop over to the nearest convenience store and get a sickeningly sweet, artificially flavored one...or you could grab some fresh fruits and vegetables and reward yourself with a delicious (and healthy!) alternative.

1 part cucumber puree

1 part cantaloupe puree

1 cup ice

3 parts club soda

1 cucumber wheel (garnish)

1 Peel one cucumber and slice one cantaloupe. Add a bit of each to a blender in approximately equal parts and blend until smooth.

2 Add the ice and club soda to the blender. Blend until the mixture achieves a slushy-like consistency. If necessary, add more ice to achieve your preferred thickness.

3 Pour into your Mason jar. Garnish with a cucumber wheel and enjoy!

Experiment with other flavors if you want! Lime or pineapple also works well with cucumber, so try using lime juice or pineapple puree in place of the cantaloupe. You can also try adding flavors such as raspberry or lemon to the recipe as it stands. Have fun with it!

Peach and Vanilla Infusion

Virgin cocktails are one thing, but why not take the concept to its logical conclusion? Flavor-infused water is the ultimate healthy mocktail. Store-bought flavored water tends to taste processed, but it's easier than you think to make your own with fresh ingredients! Try this sweet and flavorful peach and vanilla infusion to get you started. Serve a pitcher of this at your next gathering, and your friends will be asking how you did it.

½ gallon water

1 peach (sliced)

1 tsp vanilla extract

1 orange slice (per serving, garnish)

1 Pour the water into a pitcher. Slice the peach into segments and add them to the pitcher. Add the vanilla extract and stir until thoroughly mixed.

2 Place the pitcher in the fridge and allow to sit for at least an hour.

3 Serve in Mason jars, garnished with orange slices. Enjoy!

Plenty of other fruits work too: strawberry, blueberry, and orange are obvious suggestions. Feel free to add more or less vanilla extract as well, or swap it out for a flavor you feel might work even better.

CROWD-PLEASER

This water infusion is the perfect crowd-pleaser. All too often, the designated driver falls by the wayside. If you have multiple guests who can't partake of the evening's libations, give them something they can enjoy more than just regular water. As it stands, this infusion is already a fairly large batch, but whipping up more is as simple as multiplying the recipe.

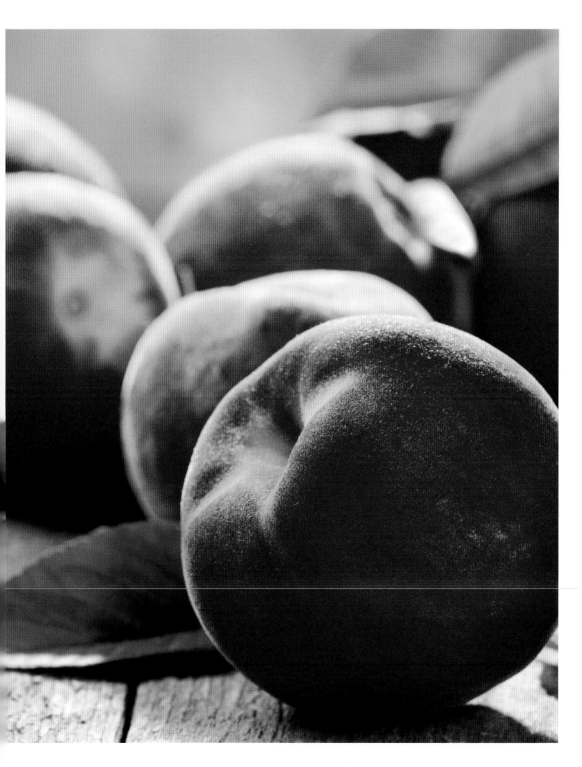

Glossary

Bourbon: Whiskey distilled from a mash of at least 51% corn. Popular in the American South.

Circle: A, thin circular slice of fruit, usually citrus. Also, a circle of cucumber. Commonly used as a garnish. Also sometimes known as a "round."

Cocktail shaker: A device to mix cocktails by shaking. When filled with ice, it is capable of quickly cooling beverages.

Infusion: Water or liquor flavored with fruits, spices, or seasonings.

Liqueur: Sweet, flavored alcoholic liquor. Usually strongly flavored and high in alcohol content.

Muddle: Lightly mash ingredients to release the flavor. Can be done with a muddler or simply the back of a spoon or other blunt instrument.

Neat: Served without ice or garnish. Usually refers to a whiskey or bourbon drink.

Scotch whiskey: Scottish whiskey matured in oak casks for over three years. Often smoky in flavor, due to the addition of peat smoke in some batches.

Simple syrup: Water infused with sugar, usually in a ratio of approximately 1:1. For instructions on how to make, see page 190.

Slice of fruit: A thin section of fruit sliced from a fruit circle. Usually ¼ or ½ of a circle. Commonly used as a garnish.

Twist: A strip of citrus rind, cut in a circular pattern around the fruit to give it a "twisted" shape.

Virgin: Nonalcoholic.

Wedge: A thick, triangular slice of fruit, commonly used as a garnish. Usually designed to be squeezed into a drink for added flavor.

Zest: The peel of a citrus fruit. Often used for flavoring or garnish. Used as a verb, zesting refers to the process of scraping off bits of the rind.

Additional Resources

BASIC BOTTLES

VODKA
Budget: Svedka
Classic: Skyy
Perfect: Grey Goose

RUM
Budget: Bacardi
Classic: Captain Morgan
Perfect: El Dorado

GIN
Budget: Seagram's
Classic: Tanqueray
Perfect: Bombay Sapphire

TEQUILA
Budget: Agavales
Classic: Jose Cuervo
Perfect: 1800

WHISKEY
Budget: Evan Williams
Classic: Maker's Mark
Perfect: Woodford Reserve

MUST-HAVE MIXERS
Sweet Vermouth
Lime Juice
Lemon Juice
Bitters
Grenadine
Simple Syrup

NICE TO HAVE
Dry Vermouth
Triple Sec
Kahlúa
Crème de Menthe
Malibu Coconut Rum
Blue Curaçao

WISH LIST
Campari
Orgeat Syrup
Flavored Bitters

About Cider Mill Press Book Publishers

Good ideas ripen with time. From seed to harvest, Cider Mill Press brings fine reading, information, and entertainment together between the covers of its creatively crafted books. Our Cider Mill bears fruit twice a year, publishing a new crop of titles each spring and fall.

"Where Good Books Are Ready for Press"

Visit us online at
cidermillpress.com

or write to us at
PO Box 454
12 Spring St.
Kennebunkport, Maine 04046